MY BABY GOT
THE YIPS

MY BABY GOT THE YIPS

*The random thoughts of an
unprofessional golfer*

RICHARD RUSSELL

First published in Great Britain
2004 by Aurum Press Ltd
25 Bedford Avenue, London WC1B 3AT

A catalogue record for this book is available from the British Library.

ISBN 1 84513 014 6

1 3 5 7 9 10 8 6 4 2
2004 2006 2008 2007 2005

Designed and typeset in Bell by Geoff Green Book Design
Printed by MPG Books, Bodmin, Cornwall

My baby got the yips.
My baby got the yips.
She goes out in 32,
But comes home in 54.

Well, I told her to see the club pro.
But she said nah-nah-nah-nah-nah no.
Have you tried the overlap grip?
Yeah … but still she got the yips.

I wrote to the Bear.
But he didn't care.
Guess he's not a Care Bear.

'Yips (My Baby Got The)'
HALF MAN HALF BISCUIT

For Trish.

Who elsh?

CONTENTS

INTRODUCTION: A QUICK BUCKET OF BALLS BEFORE TEEING OFF

I couldn't wait to be twenty-one.

I had convinced myself that a few days after my twenty-first birthday the following scenario would unfold: I would be taken aside by my parents, my father clasping me on the shoulder and looking me straight in the eye, my mother hoovering in the background. (Sorry ... hovering in the background.) And then Dad would say the magic words:

'Son, you have reached manhood. Your mother and I can now tell you that when you were born we set up a trust fund in your name, to be kept secret until you came of age. It is now worth ten million pounds.'

It never happened. Not on my twenty-first, nor my twenty-fifth. Nor my thirtieth. Nor my fortieth. In fact, I'm almost beginning to think there is no trust fund.

But while I never heard Dad say the magic words that year, I heard something else which was almost as good.

I was standing around on the first tee at Sunningdale Golf Club, swishing and swoshing away with my driver, chatting merrily with my playing partners, and every now and then doing that warming up thing where you put your club behind your shoulders and swivel about a bit for no good reason. Just like a million other golfers, on a thousand other courses, in a hundred different countries. With three big differences: Tom Watson, Seve Ballesteros and Greg Norman – my playing partners. A none too shabby bunch at any time, but this was in 1983 when, between them, they ruled the world.

My gaze wandered over to the putting green, not twenty feet away. I recognised him immediately. Indeed, he could have been a silhouette and I would still have spotted his hunched putting style. It was Jack Nicklaus; all flaxen hair and sticky-out-y elbows. He nonchalantly slotted his putt, picked it out of the cup and strolled over to the tee where the boys and I were standing.

Then it happened.

Tom Watson (five times Open winner and the only man to ever really get on Nicklaus's tits in the majors) looked over at Jack Nicklaus (eighteen majors and greatest golfer of all time in most people's eyes) and said, and I quote:

'Sorry, Jack, we're playing with Rick.'

And then I woke up and it was all a dream.

(That's the first time I've ended a story with that line since I tried it once too often in Stubbington House Lower Sixth English classes.

A shot rang out and I fell to the ground, the sniper's bullet making a small hole in my chest, but a large hole in my back. I tried to speak but no sound came.

And then I woke up and it was all a dream.')

A part of me – the part that thinks maybe it's okay to play Winter Rules in April – really doesn't want to tell you that it was a dream. Maybe, just maybe, I could have you believe that I routinely make up fourballs with golfing superstars. But the honest part of me – the part that knows just how astonishingly incompetent I am at chipping – insists I spill the beans.

Still, what a dream, eh? Not 'wet' in the usual sense but enough to have me coming over all unnecessary some twenty years down the line. (Even the dream starring Miss Kellerman, my French teacher, can't do that. And that was an experience that spectacularly disproved the commonly held belief that you can't 'taste' in dreams.)

'Sorry, Jack, we're playing with Rick.'

I tried to have it again the following night. (I was convinced this was possible because as a child I awoke one night from a barnstorming dream about UFOs and aliens, desperately needing a pee, then stumbled back into bed and deliberately slipped right back into the dream exactly where I'd left off. To this day I've never heard of anyone else performing a similar trick.)

I dug out my Dad's copy of *Golf My Way* by Jack Nicklaus, and immersed myself in it before turning out the light, but it was no good. (Well, I say no good. I didn't have the dream, but I did discover that it was a good idea to hover your driver just above the ground to make for a smoother takeaway, and that everyone should have a 'trigger', like Jack's head turn and Gary Player's knee press.)

The only thing that rankles about the whole thing is that Tom Watson called me 'Rick'. I went through a horribly misguided 'Rick' period in the late Seventies, early Eighties, thinking it made me sound cooler and more like someone that girls slept with, and now I can't shake the sound of the word spilling from Watson's lips.

My Dad had the right idea. He hated the name 'Rick' from the outset and when any of my friends would ring me at home to fix up a game the conversation would invariably progress along these lines:

DAD: Yes? Ascot 385513.

FRIEND: Oh, hello Mr Russell, is Rick there?

DAD: No I'm sorry, Rick isn't here.

FRIEND: Oh. Okay then.

DAD: My son Richard is at home, though. Would you care to speak to *him*?

FRIEND: Er … yes, that would be fine, Mr Russell.

The bit about Sunningdale Golf Club is the one part that is true. Sunningdale was, and is, my home club and, consequently a natural place to set my dream fourball. As I write, I've played my golf there for twenty-eight years; which isn't bad for someone who's forty-one. It's a wonderful place to hit a golf ball, with two (two!) world class courses, and I'm a jammy git to proclaim it as my own. Luckily, it also boasts fewer unbearable wankers amongst its membership than you might think for a club at the very heart of the golfing establishment. Offhand, I can only think of two, which isn't bad at all.

Over the years, I've gone from playing there every single day, frequently thirty-six holes, to the not-even-remotely grand tally of four solitary games last year. Two things haven't helped. One: I've moved seventy-five miles away to live in a little village in East Sussex. Two: I am now happily married to Trish, with two point nought wonderful children, Buster and Ruby.

In short, I am just another middle-aged golfer who doesn't feel he can play on the weekend. Richard Russell – The Wilderness Years.

As I write, I am disgusted to report that my last full round was over twelve weeks ago. In fact, even that doesn't count because it was a foursomes match with my Dad and I only played half the shots. So, actually, it was that game at Rye; my last full eighteen holes of golf; three-and-a-bit months ago; a quarter of a year; a season; the full metamorphosis of tadpole to frog. You get the picture.

This has been going on for a few years now, though each year seems to get marginally worse. But here's where this sob-story takes a strange and ironic turn.

I am playing the best golf of my life.

Never have I stood on a tee and felt more confident of hitting the fairway. Never have I struck my irons so crisply and Olazabal-ly. Yes, my putting is a bit on/off and, yes, my chipping remains laughable but I can still get round. My handicap is only a few decimal places away from being the lowest it's ever been; (5.6 actually, thanks for asking.) My favourite club is the 1-iron. One-iron, for Pete's sake. No one's favourite club is the 1-iron. They're devilishly difficult to hit (boasting as they do a 1:1 clubface gradient) and most sensible pros don't even carry one any more.

(Lee Trevino once held his up over his head and walked down the fairway with it, just as a lightning storm started up. 'Not even God can hit a 1-iron,' he said.)

Any day now the 1-iron will go the way of the baffy, cleek, and spoon, and I'll be the last person to carry it, drawing whispered asides from strangers as I pull it out on the practice range.

(Actually, I lie. That will never happen because I never practice. Golf courses are beautiful and a pleasure to tread; driving ranges are ugly, you have to play off mats, and I always play rubbish on them, which rather seems to defeat the purpose.)

In short, I am more in love with the game of golf than I have ever been, even though I am playing less of it than I have ever played. On the one hand I'm exasperated, and on the other (the one wearing an all-weather glove) I'm well aware that it is my enforced absence from the game that has finally made me appreciate the joy and wonder of it. When I do venture out I am so intoxicated by the sights, the sounds, the challenge, the exercise, the chat, the scribble of pencil on card, those comfy new double carrying straps, the amazing taste of Lucozade Orange Sport, white wooden tee pegs, the comforting knowledge that golf isn't fattening, and the urge to drink ginger beer shandy in the clubhouse afterwards that … well, dammit, it makes me glad to be alive and I don't care who knows it.

All of which is in stark contrast to the Jekyll and Hyde golfer I used to know whose piss-poor attitude brought golfing misfortune raining down upon him every bit as much as his over-active legs, collapsed hands at the top, and destructive in-to-out thrash: a golfer whose moody sulks must have spoiled countless games for his long-suffering playing partners. (Sorry Mark T. Sorry Scotty. Sorry Mark C. Forgive me, I knew not what I was doing.)

And so to this book, and what is intended to be a beguiling

mixture of golfing autobiography (unauthorised), golfing philosophy, and bumper book of golfing fun (amazing tales; the greatest golfer you've never heard of; prodigious sausage-eating; etc).

The golfing autobiography part is, some might say, a bit of a cheek. I am not a professional golfer and I am not a public figure. (Though I have played with Tom Watson, Seve Ballesteros and Greg Norman, don't forget.) But I am a golfer. I have paid my dues. I have shanked, topped, thinned, fatted (?!), yipped and choked. Also, when the golfing gods have deemed fit; birdied, eagled, backspinned, cut the corner off doglegs, and holed everything in sight.

I have, while representing Rye (my second club) in a foursomes match and chipping onto the final green, clipped the side of my ball while taking a practice swing, sending it twenty feet further away from the hole to the ice-cold bemusement of my partner. I have participated in a unique fourball whose respective gross scores on the (blue tees) par-five second hole at Sunningdale were par; birdie; eagle; and albatross. (Congratulations Mark T on your fabulous albatross. Guess who got the lowly par?) I have, upon facing a horrible chip shot over a bunker, off a bare lie, and with only a few feet of green to work with, taken a 3-iron and, on a hunch, punched it into the bunker, run it up the face, popped it an inch onto the green, curled it down the slope to just a foot-and-a-half from the hole … and then missed the putt.

The average round of your average golfer is, I would argue, far more interesting and entertaining than the latest 67 from your sweet-swinging, logo-wearing, glove-remov-

ing tour pro. Even when they're rubbish they're good.
To misquote Bobby Jones, 'they play a monotonous, robotic
game with which we are not familiar'.

(Glorious exception: Colin Montgomerie at the 2002
Open. Begins with a 74 to risk missing the cut; follows it
with a course record 64 to spark foolish talk of his first
major; weighs in with an 84 to put paid to the whole pre-
posterous idea. 74–64–84. Now that's symmetrical genius.)

So, on behalf of all Sunday morning golfers everywhere,
from hackers to scratch-ers, I'd like to twitter on about the
glorious game for a while. What say we head out towards
the first tee and continue chatting? I've bought some
Titleist Super Pro 'Big Boy' XL 59s; I've stocked up on the
yummy Lucozade Orange Sport; I've enjoyed an aimless
two-minute practice putt; I've got my key swing thought
for the day (hold the club with only the same pressure as
you would hold a dove); and I've had my customary last-
minute bowel evacuation.

The sun is out, the course is clear and if we hurry we can
be off before that fourball over there. So c'mon, it'll be fun.

Oh, and at some point I'll be giving away the secret of
golf.

If you're interested.

CHAPTER ONE: DADDY, WHERE DO SHANKS COME FROM?

I t was the tees that did it for me, rather than the game itself. Blue, red, yellow, white, and occasionally a really pretty lime green. And they were all over the place. Most of them were broken but that didn't bother me. Into my pocket they were stuffed as I trailed after my Dad round some long-forgotten golf course. We were on holiday, and I was eight; he was playing golf, and I was tagging along.

Oh, the excitement of arriving at every new hole and scouring the grass for these colourful golfing droppings. Irrefutable evidence that others had been there before, balanced their little white balls on tiny pegs, smashed them with a club, and charged off after them not knowing what precious jewels they were leaving behind.

Even then I preferred the wooden tees. The plastic ones were okay for holding between your teeth and chomping on like some kind of kiddy cigar, but there was something much more thrilling about the wooden ones and how they ended up all bashed and splintered. They had died heroically, and were now consigned to the dirt, casualties of golf. Well, not if I could help it.

I suppose at some point I must have expressed a desire to actually hit a ball, rather than just tidy up the course, for I was soon joining Dad for the occasional game at his new club – Puttenham, near Guildford. (Good name.) For a nipper, the first hole had the most insanely difficult tee shot. You had to clear the brow of a big hill that seemed about 500 yards away and, at the same time, avoid a huge great tree on the hill, directly between you and the fairway.

It was an impossible shot for a shortarse like me and while, eventually, this was the hole where I made my first ever par, it was also almost certainly the hole where I said my first 'fuck', 'shit', 'bollocks' and 'wank' as well.

Not within earshot of Dad, though. He is not a fan of bad language, and has only once ever uttered a swearword in my presence. It was a good one, mind – 'Bugger' – which was pretty strident for my father, seeing as how in his mind 'to bugger' is right up there with 'to rip out a still-beating heart with your bare hands'. The thing is, he's quite right about swearing; it's not clever, it's just coarse and unnecessary. It sounds right when Billy Connolly curses; it suits him. It sounds right when Samuel L. Jackson swears in *Pulp Fiction*, but not when I do it; even if I have just missed a two-footer by a full ball's width. So I try not to, either on the course or off. As expressive and satisfying as it is to eff and blind, it's also ugly – especially when it issues forth from the mouths of well-spoken home counties folk whose hands have never seen a decent day's work in their lives; let alone a callous-inducing session on the driving range.

Dad and I went back to Puttenham recently; about thirty years after our last game there. We don't get to play together too often these days, and with him turning seventy recently it seemed like a good thing to do. We played the bonkers first hole with a dopey grin on our face and then, to our mounting horror, wandered confused and disappointed round the rest of the course. There wasn't one single hole that rang a bell. It was like we were playing a completely different course, only one that had cleverly managed to borrow Puttenham's first hole, and clubhouse. It was only while playing the eighteenth that the warm glow of recognition returned and we found ourselves once again strolling pleasantly down memory lane. It was a short stroll, mind, seeing as how it's a mid-iron par-three.

Afterwards, we spoke with the steward and mentioned that we used to play there in the early 1970s. 'Oh really,' he said 'We had it completely re-designed a few years back. It's a much better test of golf these days, don't you think?' We slugged back our half of bitter, wolfed down our prawn baguette with a Marie Rose sauce; and drove away sharpish, not wanting to sully the memory any further. They say you should never go back. They're right.

In 1975 the Russell family moved a couple of miles to a house right next to Sunningdale Golf Club, even though, upon first being asked what we thought of the idea, my elder brother Paul and I burst into tears and beat the carpet with our fists. I soon realised that everything was all right, however, when I discovered that the back gate opened onto the practice ground, not fifty paces from the clubhouse. (At that time I wasn't aware that I was a congenital non-practiser.) When we moved in I was amazed to stumble across a golf ball in the grass of our new, somewhat overgrown garden, even though it was exactly level with the practice tees – the only place it could have come from. Heaven knows how anyone could have been bad enough to have hit it there. A right-hander would have had to hit it through his own legs, and a left-hander would have had to shank it eighty yards over a hedge and at an exact angle of ninety degrees.

A few weeks later, my father heard that Sunningdale were holding a teaching clinic, given by their resident professional Clive Clark, for prospective junior members (or 'Cadets' as they decided to call them.) By chance, the club had just decided to set up a junior section and this was their first clinic, to get an idea of how the local juniors played. I had just turned thirteen and, fortuitously, that was the age you had to be to attend the clinic. (It would have been cool if Paul had come too but, after a couple of lessons, he had already decided that golf was not his thing. This was a shame but, on the other hand, while I spent all my teenage years wandering about in fields, fighting a hook, he spent all of his with a dazzling succession of beautiful girlfriends, so good call, bruv.)

The clinic was quite interesting. Clive Clark holed a bunker shot. I didn't.

They say you need to be in the right place at the right time, and I was all that, and more. Within weeks of joining, and really only thanks to having a good eye for a ball, I had got my first handicap of 11, and a few months after that had got it down to 10, a handicap low enough to allow me, under Cadet rules, to play whenever I wanted.

What, in effect, this meant was that while pillars of the establishment and captains of industry were forced to wait in line for years and years till their membership to Sunningdale came through (no matter who they knew, or how much they were prepared to pay), some freckle-faced, side-parted whippersnapper had sneaked in the back door and was playing two of the greatest courses in the land, all for the princely sum of £20 a year.

It was scandalous. And I loved it.

I have to say that this is one of the most endearing things about Sunningdale. It just doesn't seem to feel the need to flex its muscles by charging a fortune. It is the complete opposite of its glitzier neighbour just three miles up the road – the Wentworth Golf Swimming Tennis Spa Driving Range Restaurant and Country Club. Sunningdale's subscriptions are less than half of Wentworth's and it's perfectly happy just being a golf club, with no immediate plans for world domination or cracking the Forbes Top Ten Business List.

The Sunningdale members were warm and welcoming to me and my teenage cohorts, and I wasn't ever aware of any animosity towards us. This is pretty incredible when you think about it. After seventy-five years of having the place to themselves, suddenly there were all these snot-nosed kids running around, cluttering up the fairways and the putting green and, saints preserve us, even the bar. You'd think they would have resented our overnight arrival, but not a bit of it. Another reason why I say that Sunningdale, despite its lofty status in the world of golf, is one of the friendliest golf clubs you could ever visit.

One of the highlights of the year for a teenage Sunningdale golfer was the annual Members and Cadets match. Again, to their credit, this wasn't a Them versus Us affair, in an attempt to grind us pesky kids into the dust and remind us of our place, but a joining of forces in teams, each pairing trying to score the most Stableford points.

We loved it but at the same time dreaded it, for it wasn't just one or two Colonel Bufton-Tuftons who would turn out (old boys who we could hugely impress with our prodigious length, even when we didn't connect properly), but the cream of the club's players. And some of these guys were extra-thick double cream made from Guernsey cows, raised in the Channel Islands on a rich carpet of verdant grass known locally as Lush Wilton.

(Sunningdale is sometimes referred to as having the most single-figure players of any club in Britain. I'm not sure about that but I remember a little while ago, out of interest, examining the alphabetical member's list in the porch and counting how many people were lower than my handicap of 6, figuring that, technically at least, I had to be one of the best players in the club. I stopped counting, somewhat crestfallen, when the figure reached 100 and I hadn't even got past 'M'.)

This particular year, when I was fifteen, the two members in my group were about as stellar as they come. The first was a friendly fellow called Mike Hughesdon who played off scratch. (The same Mike Hughesdon who would go on to become one of the BBC's on-course reporters. You know, the guy who stands over some player's ball in the light rough and whispers into a microphone how the young Swede has got a bit of a clover-y lie, and how he'll be lucky to make the cross bunkers … only for the willowy Swede to despatch it to the heart of the green with an easy 6-iron.

Interestingly, the same job that Clive Clark, the clinic-giving Sunningdale pro, also had. Or not interestingly, as the case may be.) The other member, and my partner on the day, was an ex-Walker Cup player, generally regarded as being one of the finest ball strikers ever to represent his country.

Hey-ho.

I figured I could probably cobble it round without embarrassing myself too much, after all, this was a couple of years after I'd joined and I knew my way round the course okay, but I was in a real quandary over what club to take on the first tee. There were loads of people milling around, watching the groups go off and while I was a pretty wild player anyway, I was ridiculously wild off the first tee, before my swing had had any chance to settle into some kind of natural muscular order. (It's not as if I was grooving it on the practice ground beforehand, after all.) Finally, I decided that discretion was the better part of valour, and that a nice 2-iron would do the job. Or perhaps I thought that cowardice was the better part of humiliation. Anyway, I was definitely going to hit an iron for safety. It might go a wee bit off line but at least the houses over the other side of the trees weren't in any danger.

Sadly … pathetically … I duffed it; the ball only just bobbing over the end of the tee, after a swing officially timed by Accurist at 0.26 seconds.

The Sunningdale members don't play that rule where you have to finish the hole with your penis out if you fail to reach the ladies tee with your drive, but I think even that humiliation couldn't have made me more embarrassed than I felt at that moment. Smiling weakly and offering up some lame comment about 'taking an iron for danger', I walked after the rest of the group. You could tell they were wondering what the hell they'd let themselves in for.

On the second hole, a long, difficult par-four, my Walker Cup partner unleashed a huge behemoth of a drive, drawing it round the slight dogleg for extra distance and maximum gorgeousness. Looking like he couldn't love himself any more if he tried, he tossed the driver to his caddie, turned to us and said, 'Well, I just don't hit them any better than that.'

Fuck it, I thought. Whatever happens it can't be worse than the first; I'll take my driver and pray I don't cock it up. Fuelled by fear, I hit an absolute smoker. Amazingly, it even went straight and by the time it had finished rolling it was a good ten yards past him; the longest drive I had ever hit on that hole.

He was not happy – unlike Mike Hughesdon, who laughed so hard he had to put on his waterproof trousers. And while I wouldn't say my partner didn't talk to me for the rest of the round, relations were certainly strained, and from that moment on we didn't quite gel as a team in the way I had hoped.

(Yes, I know … I swore just then. The thing is, I've just discovered it works much better in print. I think it's because you can't hear my voice uttering the oath. So while this won't suddenly turn into an Irvine Welsh novel, I can't promise it won't happen again.)

Can I just say that I am well aware that when it comes to having the opportunity to play golf, I was born with a silver spoon in my golf bag. Not only did I have the best inland course in the country at the bottom of my garden, but I also went to a minor public school in Dorset that actually had a nine-hole golf course in its grounds. The school was Milton Abbey, near Blandford, and the course was designed by Peter Alliss, whose son Gary went there a few years before me.

It had three par-fours, and half the par-threes needed a good whack with a short iron, so it was by no means a piddly little pitch-and-putt affair. I loved that course, even though it was, to this day, the scene of my biggest golfing disappointment.

Jim Leggett was God. He was by far and away the best golfer in the school and, when only sixteen, set the course record at the nearby Isle of Purbeck. In my first year there, I drew him in the school Knockout Cup, and sure enough, with three of the eighteen holes to go I was 3 down, but bugger me if I didn't conjure up a couple of birdies, win all three holes, and take the match down the nineteenth.

I was getting excited now, with visions of me being hoisted onto the shoulders of my classmates and paraded round the school to wild cheering and the throwing in the air of hats. But I forced myself to stay in the present (as the pros say) and even employed some course management for my tee shot down the first extra hole. It was a par-four and at over 300 yards it was the longest hole on the course. Its biggest hazard was a lush, overgrown patch of grass and reeds in the middle of the fairway, about 200 yards down the hole, which was the site of a natural spring and was always just a mass of vegetation.

The big danger for me was that a good drive would occasionally run into it. (I was only thirteen, remember.)

But not this day, nosireee. I was canny; I was savvy; I was displaying maturity beyond my years. I figured an easy 4-iron would lay up perfectly and put the pressure right back in the lap of the great, but only human, Jim Leggett. I struck it beautifully – too beautifully – and, to my horror, it stayed in the air forever till it bounced once and hopped straight into the crap. But … but … but. I didn't understand what had happened. I'd never got anywhere near that rough with a 4-iron before. Had we played off the Ladies tee? Had I got confused between my 4-iron and my driver? Had the ball caught some freak air pocket?

I learned a valuable lesson that day. It was a double chemistry lesson about how, when excited, stressed or nervous, the human body produces a hormone called *adrenaline*, secreted from two glands sitting just above each kidney. This surge of adrenaline makes our heart pump faster, widens the air passages in the lungs, and tightens up the blood vessels, leading to the body feeling more alert and physically capable, and performance being enhanced. Thanks to adrenaline, mothers can lift cars off their children, and thirteen-year-old golfers can tonk a 4-iron over 200 yards.

Needless to say, I lost the hole and the match.

For the next couple of years, Jim continued to do great things with a golf ball and everyone reckoned he would eventually turn pro. Instead, he stopped devoting himself to golf, to devote himself to God. And nothing wrong with that, you might think; except, while God doesn't have anything in particular against golf, he does have something against his flock doing it on a Sunday, so that was that for Jim's pro career.

Over ten years after I left Milton Abbey, me and another Old Boy got in touch with Jim and persuaded him to have a game with us. We met on a Saturday and had a pleasant threeball round the New Zealand Club near Woking, in Surrey. Jim still had his clubs but he hadn't played a round for years. He had a 73.

Mr. Stewart-Henry taught history and didn't like me. This was a shame because he was also the master in charge of golf. He was a small, ruddy-faced man with a belly that didn't go with his slight frame (imagine a slighter, smaller, more scowling Kenneth Clarke). I was in the school golf team from my first year to my last (1975 to 1980), which was pretty rare, and in my final year I was captain. Put like that it doesn't seem like he had any beef with me at all, but Stewfart-Henry had the last laugh. He didn't give me my golf colours. For the captain of any of the school's senior teams, in any sport, to not get their colours was unheard of, but Stewtwat-Henry obviously didn't agree.

He was also in charge of the First XI hockey, and steadfastly ignored me for selection at right back, despite regular exhortations from the rest of the team. There is, of course, the possibility that I wasn't good enough, but all the evidence suggested otherwise, and anyway I'd hate to let that get in the way of a good grudge.

Should I ever be in a position to make a benevolent donation to the school, I think I might have to give it only on condition that they finally hand me my golf colours. I'd only need a small ceremony, nothing too grand, and if they could wheel my colours out on a trolley, clasped between the teeth of a prostrate Stewshit-Henry, that would be a nice touch. I might even add another nought to the cheque.

Now, I know what you're thinking. You're thinking, Richard, didn't your best ever round have something to do with your old school? Oh, what the heck – I wasn't going to mention it but yes, you're right. Ten years after I left Milton Abbey I organised an Old Boys golf day at Royal Mid-Surrey.

I shot a 66.

A 66 with a dropped shot at the last, as well.

So while it could have been even better, I had to be satisfied with a 66.

What I particularly liked about my score that day (66) was that it happened in the company of people I very rarely play with, so to this day (thanks to that 66) they must think that I am one shit-hot dude on a golf course.

Easy mistake to make, mind.

I did shoot a 66.

Back at Sunningdale, I was thoroughly enjoying this Cadet lark. I only got to play in the school holidays but made up for that by being up at the club every day of them.

Most days would follow the same pattern: beginning with a leisurely roll-up around lunchtime for eighteen holes on the Old Course. (It had to be lunchtime for we rarely rose before midday, and it had to be the Old Course for, as pathetic as it sounds, it was easier than the New. What fearless golfing buccaneers we were.)

One lunchtime, I remember, I inadvertently fell foul of that eternal golf club truth; that while all members are equal, some are more equal than others.

Possibly the most distinguished member when I joined was a man called Gerald Micklem. A former captain of The Royal and Ancient, he was an old man by the late 1970s but was known throughout the golfing world as being one of the foremost authorities on the game. (He was also one of the very few British members at Augusta, and me and the boys had this ridiculous notion that just because we used to say 'Good morning, Mr Micklem' to him, he would invite us out for a game there at some point.) One day I was at the bar and decided to order a spot of lunch.

'Could I have a toasted cheese and onion sandwich, please.' I said, in a squeaky voice.

'Oh no, I'm afraid not, sir,' came the reply. 'Mr Micklem doesn't like onion.'

It was an answer that appeared to bear no relation to the question I'd just asked, but after a few bewildering seconds, the penny dropped.

Mr Micklem didn't like onion, so they didn't have any onion, so no one got onion.

Blimey. Luckily, Mr Micklem quite liked ham.

Somedays, if we were playing in the afternoon, we'd arrange to meet up on the first tee, and even though I only lived a hundred paces from the first tee, I was nearly always the last to arrive. This would confuse the others.

'But it stands to reason,' I'd say. 'If you're late, you guys can simply hurry up, whereas if I'm late, I'm already here.' Watching someone stare blankly at you with an open mouth and a confused, dog-like tilt of the head is a disquieting experience, but even though no one ever bought into my theory, I stand by it.

After the round we'd loll about with cooling drinks, smoking Marlboro, being witty, and imagining our names on the various competition boards that flanked the main bar. (For me and my oldest pal, Mark Trickett, Marlboro was the cigarette of choice. This was ever since we heard a rumour that the reason it was such a strong smoke was because they put iron filings in it. If we were going to smoke, only the worst-for-you cigarette would do.)

Once, in a moment of impetuous puffery, I bought a cigar: a cheroot, no less. I didn't know what a cheroot was but it seemed full of Moroccan promise, so I settled into a red leather armchair and puffed away on it like a Bond baddie. Until I went green. Figuring that red and green would clash, I staggered home, somehow managing not to throw up on the practice range. I passed my mother on the stairs; a trusting woman who did not know, and would not have been pleased to know, that I smoked. She looked at me, startled, like I was the undead.

'I'm not feeling so good, Mum … think I'll have a bit of a lie-down. Must have been all that cigarette smoke in the bar … horrible habit … must have got to me.'

Truly, I was a pathetic, low-down dog.

One of the oft-overlooked pleasures of being a teenager and playing a lot of golf is the fact that a clubhouse is basically a pub with showers. So not only could we play golf and have a laugh, we could smoke and drink with impunity. We weren't stupid, mind: we didn't actually get drunk, and it's not like we ordered whisky and sodas, but as long as you ordered drinks that didn't sound particularly potent, you could enjoy all the pleasures of alcohol without risking any of the mocking laughter of landlords. It might sound obvious but a pint of shandy is *half a pint of beer*. Four of those and you'd racked up a couple of pints of the hard stuff, all the while seemingly ordering a drink no more hallucinatory than orange squash.

Lager and lime was another good one. Ninety-three per cent alcohol but it still sounded a wussy drink, perfect for an innocent-sounding order. Top Deck (that fantastic 1970s fizzy pop) did a superb can of Lager and Lime (*'WITH REAL LAGER!'*) that you could drink if you were barely past babyhood, so how could anyone bat an eye when a strapping, six-foot fifteen-year-old ordered one?

And then there was the ultimate teenage golfer's drink – Pimm's No. 1 Cup, the original alcopop. If you'd won a couple of quid out on the course that day, then a gin Pimm's was the business; 50p for a half; a pound for a pint, and surprisingly alcoholic. Plus, it got expertly made in front of you, like it was a cocktail or something. How sophisticated was that? All me and the boys needed was a sharp tuxedo and shiny brogues and we would have been … well, spotty tossers in tuxedos, actually, but squiffy spotty tossers, so who cares?

CHAPTER TWO: **THE FAB FOURBALL**

Once I'd realised that golf was a sport where you didn't have to wear shorts, and I'd begun playing it regularly, my recollections are that it went from one extreme to another in no time at all. To start with I struggled to reach the par-fours in two, but then my next memory, as though it was just the following week, is of whacking merry hell out of the ball.

Over the course of the next few years I played with plenty of other Cadets, but there was undoubtedly a hard-core fourball.

Mark Trickett had been my best mate since I was eight, and had joined Sunningdale just as I had. Tall, slim and blond, he was like an early, mid-1970s version of another Mark – Mark Roe. Mark (Trickett) had a flat sweeping swing that was all hands but served him just fine, and he also had the most extraordinary ability to hit a good shot off the first tee. For everyone else the first tee is an unholy plinth of nerves and trepidation, leading to some of the fastest, jerkiest swings ever winced at, yet Mark would effortlessly ease one down the middle of the fairway, regardless of whether it was a competition, or a match, or he had a hangover, or whether there was anyone watching. Sadly,

the put-your-house-on-it excellence of this one shot did
not always guarantee a further eighteen holes of the same.
Eventually, poor putting would drive Mark from the game,
à la Hogan, but not before, aged twenty-two, he did the one
thing that the rest of us, to our eternal shame, have never
managed. He got his name on a big board in the main bar:

FOUNDER'S SINGLES. M. W. H. TRICKETT.

HANDICAP 12.

And to think, Mark was a full year younger than Seve
was when he won his first Masters.

The Founders Singles is the matchplay knockout event
of the year and to win it you had to prevail in seven matches
spread over two weekends. Anyone who was anyone entered
it, as well as anyone who wasn't really anyone, but thought
they might as well have a bash. Which is where Mark and
the rest of us came in. It was usually won by the grizzled,
hardened golfers who played for not inconsiderable sums of
money, and could keep their game together under pressure.
It was not meant to be won by someone with an abominable
short game who was only used to playing for toasted
teacakes, and who was all but blind in one eye following an
unfortunate accident with a dart when he was a child.

But in much the same way that plucky West Ham, from
the old second division, marched inexorably to victory in
the 1980 FA Cup, as if propelled by an invisible, Disney-
esque, every-dog-has-its-day force, so did Mark despatch all
and sundry, as though he did this sort of thing all the time.
He had a few scares on the way, mind.

In the quarter-finals his opponent was two up with
three to play, and safely on the difficult sixteenth of the Old

in two shots. Game over, surely? Somehow, Mark won on the nineteenth. In the semi-final he had a three foot putt at the last for victory – and missed it. They headed down the first again, a par-five, and Mark's opponent, having messed the hole up something rotten, proceeded to chip in for a birdie. Only for Mark, in his new Johnny Miller guise, to roll in his thirty-foot eagle putt. How's them Dunlop 65s?

To the twenty or so spectators, the final proved something of an anti-climax, as Mark elegantly swept to a 7 and 6 victory against one of the more elderly members who had defied his age, and the odds, to reach the final, but was now a spent force. I could see their point, fairytale ending and all that but, frankly, I couldn't give a fig. My mate was The Man, and anyway, I had another reason for wanting his opponent to fail.

As it happens I had met him in an earlier round, just when I was beginning to think that maybe this was going to be *my* year. I always hated drawing anyone over sixty-five in the Founders. They knocked it 180 yards dead straight every time; they had a short game to make you gasp; and whenever they holed a putt of any length, they apologised, which only made things worse. Even today, I can vividly recall one old boy urging me to keep my pecker up, and trying gamely to convince me that anything could still happen, as I stood on the fifteenth tee, dormy-four down, mere moments before he despatched me 5 and 3. To a man, these golfing pensioners were wily, battle-hardened and thoroughly pleasant and gentlemanly to boot. And I hated them all.

Mark's guy was equally hard to beat. My match with him had gone to the eighteenth and, with the pressure escalating, I hit first. My drive was so far left, and so big, that it cleared the fairway, cleared the rough to the left of the fairway, cleared the first fairway that ran adjacent to the final hole, and went deep into the trees on the other side of the first fairway. In its own way this was quite a singular feat, just not what I wanted to do at that particular moment. There was a second or two of silence, then it was broken by my silver-haired adversary. 'My God, that was an *awful* shot.' he said. (Not, 'Hard luck.' Not, 'Must have been the wind.' Not, 'Still … good hit.' Not even respectful silence for the death of my chances.) Needless to say, in ten more minutes I was shaking his throat. Hand. Whatever.

So it was with shameful relish that I celebrated Mark's remorseless pounding into the dust of his plucky, septuage-narian opponent. A few months later, Captain's Day arrived and The Fab Four attended their one and only annual prize-giving ceremony so as to duly acclaim our new champion. When it came to the Founder's Singles the beaten finalist was announced first, to huge applause from the assembled crowd; including us. After all, the old boy had had an amazing run and it was, in all probability, his last moment in the spotlight's glare.

'And so to the winner of the Founder's Singles Cup … Mark Trickett.' As Mark got up and shyly made his way to the smiling Captain, Scott, Mark and I exploded into raucous applause: a merry noise made even louder by the pathetic muted applause that the rest of the room gave him, obviously disappointed that the other guy hadn't won. Well fuck that for a game of soldiers, we thought, so the three of us stood up and clapped still louder. We clapped him all the way back to his seat. The highest handicapper to win the Founder's Singles for twenty-five years; a lovely bloke and one of our own.

Mark lives and works in Greece now, and has just started a family with his beautiful Brazilian wife, Patricia. (In a neat bit of symmetry, the same name as my lovely wife, too.) He only plays at Sunningdale once every couple of years these days, dusting off his clubs to crack the inevitable beauty off the first tee, followed by a ragged but enjoyable round in the company of his old muckers.

But as irregularly as he visits these days, one thing remains immutable.

His name is on the board every single day. You bloody beauty.

Scott Alexander was, and probably still is, the golfer we secretly wanted to be. There was something reassuringly steady about his game and when, on the first tee, the balls were thrown in the air, you couldn't help but hope that your reject Commando was the one to have nestled closest to his Green Flash. The rest of us were birdie/bogey kind of golfers – too mercurial, too unpredictable, too shit. While we undoubtedly had our moments, Scott could do the one thing that we could not – score well when not appearing to be playing well.

In temperament, playing style, and (uncanny) appearance, Scott was the David Gilford of the Cadets. (Scott Simpson was another phlegmatic, slow-swinging contender for comparison and, pleasingly, had the added bonus of boasting the same first name, but he was also prematurely

grey, which would paint a wholly misleading mental picture
of the young Alexander. I did briefly toy with an Eddie
Pollard connection, which would score highly for the correct era and similarly unspectacular but effective game – no
offence Scotty – but in the end I felt he was simply too
jowly. So David Gilford it is. I can live with it if you can.)

The comparison with Gilford is really not as rude as it
sounds. True, if you took a bunch of golf-mad kids and
asked them to make up an imaginary Ryder Cup team, there
wouldn't be too many jumping up and going, 'Ooh, ooh, I'll
be David Gilford,' but for a while there, back in the
Nineties, he was impressively inscrutable and the man most
likely to be voted (by me, anyway) The-One-Person-You'd-
Bet-Your-Life-On-To-Get-A-Par-If-He-Absolutely-Had-
To. Frankly, I was always surprised that his star never
shone brighter.

The crucial area where he and Scott differed however,
was their backswing. Gilford's was taut, powerful and at
ninety degrees to the ground. Scott's was so long and
overswung that it pointed straight down *at* the ground
instead. Astonishingly, it didn't seem to affect his game.
Indeed, on the occasions that he did force himself to shorten
it to a mere few degrees past the horizontal, he would end
up all out of whack, and spray it about like a mad woman's
spittle. Strangely, the rest of us never really mentioned it.
It was like a large, red facial birthmark: he knew it was
there, we knew it was there, but there seemed little point
bringing it up in polite conversation when it didn't seem to
be making any difference to anything. In his early twenties,
he went off and had it seen to – golf lessons as laser treat-

ment – and came back, new and not in the least bit improved. No better, no worse, just less likely to have the clubhead fracture his left ankle on every backswing.

The first time I met Scott I remember coming home that evening and mentioning to my Mum that I'd played with a nice bloke that day.

'Oh yes,' she said. 'What's his name?'

I paused, with furrowed brow. 'No idea.' I finally replied.

She gave me an exasperated look that spoke volumes. Volume One: an incomprehension that I could spend, all told, five or six hours in someone's company and not glean this most basic piece of information. Volume Two: a shoulder-slumping frustration at my dreamy ways. And Volume Three: a parent's very real concern at their offspring's ability to get on in life in any way, shape or form.

While the rest of us were pretty long hitters, Scott was not. He didn't so much Grip It And Rip It, as Squeeze It And Ease It, obviously not understanding that the point of a long par-four is not to par or birdie it, but to see if you can one day get on it with a drive and a pitching wedge. It is to his credit that continually being twenty or thirty yards behind the rest of us did not seem to make him strain for extra length at all. Perhaps that was because he was on the fairway.

Mark Courage was a left-hander. Shunned by society, a freak and an outcast, he was in danger of only ever playing by himself and, as such, having no standing in the game. He seemed a cheery sort of bloke though, so we took pity on this poor, wrong-swinging wretch and let him be in our gang.

Let's be clear about one thing; the left-handed golf swing is one of nature's foulest abominations, beaten only by raw, swollen monkey bottoms. And one of God's particularly good jokes is to bestow upon most of its unfortunate exponents a silky-sweet swing that would otherwise have us purring in appreciation, were it only performed by right-minded, right-handed folk. Wrapped up as it is, however, in a hideous cloak of wrong-ness, we can but rush to cover the eyes of small children, while we ourselves recoil and cower like vampires caught in dawn's early light.

It's not left-handed sportsmen per se that are such an affront to our sensibilities – picture the gorgeous loose-limbed beauty of a David Gower or a Bjorn Borg – just golfers. Sometimes, they can be saved; a right-handed club superglued into the palm of their left hand before the age of ten usually does it. Other times you just need to take them aside and quietly inform them that even a young Ben Hogan stopped playing left-handed when he saw how twatting stupid he looked.

I think it says much for our innate goodness that Scott, Mark T and I were happy to invite Mark into our bosom of golf and permanently expose ourselves to his unsettling swing and the very real risk that something might rub off. On the other hand, it also says much about Mark that he could rise above the whispered comments and averted gazes to become something very close to a proper golfer.

He was a dashing player, right from the word go. While the rest of us would tip up in fairly tatty attire, albeit strictly regulation, Mark would be smart, sharp and colour co-ordinated to the nth degree. He had different shoes, for instance; not for the conditions, but for the trousers he might be wearing that day. Sometimes his shirts veered a shade too close to the kind of mottled atrocity worn by USPGA tour pros you've never heard of, but that was all. (Picture an unsettling shade of swirly avocado green mixed with swirly creamy white – like those gloopy oil patterns you used to be shown at the cinema before the film started.)

It may be an obvious choice but, in all but paunch, Mark was every bit the Phil Mickelson. A naturally attacking, risk-taking player, he would sometimes come a cropper but equally, he had the capacity (and the gall) to pull off some incredible shots.

He also played the greatest hole of golf I shall probably ever witness. (See Chapter 4 for details.)

(Special mention here for Nick Maclean, one of the other Cadets I played with, and someone who was brilliant company on a golf course. In almost every regard, Nick was just a bit more '-er' than we were. He was taller, stronger, faster swinging, wilder, spectacular-er, and much as it pains me to admit it … longer. The purest striker of a golf ball I have ever played with, he would crunch steeply down onto it from on high and send it, literally, anywhere. Like a 9-handicap version of Seve Ballesteros, circa 1979, he was both hugely talented and totally rubbish, which lead to some extraordinary exploits. Once, on the short par-four ninth of the Old, he hit one of his usual 300-yard drives, but about sixty degrees right into no-man's-trees. Muttering away, he teed up another. Four minutes later, he tapped in the subsequent six-footer for a regulation Maclean par. The

laughing cavalier of golf, he went to live in New York about
ten years ago, and I miss him.)

There were a number of reasons why the four of us
clumped together. I knew Mark T from way back anyway,
and it undoubtedly helped that we were all pretty much the
same handicap, but the clincher I think was that we weren't
really into the gambling side of things. I say we … it was
the other three that weren't, and I just had the good sense
to realise that playing most of my golf with thoroughly
agreeable people who wouldn't resent it if I hit the odd
good shot, would be a more pleasant experience than
battling it out against the high rollers, week in, week out.

Sunningdale is famous for being a gambling club. The
main game favoured involves a fiendish little rascal called a
'press', which is basically just a great way to increase the
stakes as you play. What happens is that whenever anyone
goes two-up their opponent has the option of starting
another game from that point, to run alongside the first
one, for half the original stake. Then, the next time someone wins two holes without reply, the other person can
start a third match, the score in each game changing
accordingly; and so on, and so on, world without end, amen.

If it sounds complicated, it isn't really. Let's say you're
playing me for a tenner and you go two up after three holes,
I would then press you and start up another game with a
five pound stake. So, after three holes the score is 'Two –
Flat'. (Two holes to you, and flat on the first press.)

Then, let's say I won the next two. The score would
now be 'Flat' in the main match, 'Two' (to me) in the first

press, and 'Flat' again, because you've now pressed me on the first press and we've started another match, again for five pounds.

Ermm … okay, it is a bit complicated, but even I picked it up pretty quickly and I can't pronounce 'almond'. Everyone plays presses at The Dale*; the only things that vary being the original stake and how gung-ho you are with it.

I soon learnt an interesting side-effect of the press, though. Winning the game is not the point; which is an interesting concept. I remember once, as a Cadet, playing someone more familiar with pressing, and losing twenty quid despite soundly despatching him 4 and 3. I had failed to grasp the fundamental tenet of the game – *all that matters are the last three or four holes.* You see, what I've haven't mentioned are the byes on both the match and the presses (bye: a chance to start another match as soon as either party has lost the first one), all of which serve to make the closing holes a dizzying blur of Ups, Downs and Flats, where one missed three-footer can affect half-a-dozen different games.

It is no exaggeration to say that you can walk up the last positioned as follows: Three, One, One, Three, One, Flat, Flat, Two, Flat, Flat, Flat.

*I've just made up that name. No one has ever called it 'The Dale' but I was getting a bit tired of writing 'Sunningdale' in full each time. On reflection, I don't like it, but I think I'll leave it in just in case it gets picked up and takes off in a big way, as can sometimes happen. That way, historians can trace its origins all the way back to this very book and it might be accorded some much needed influence and gravitas.

And that's just the main fourball match. If you were feeling particularly bullish, there's every chance you've also taken on your two opponents in individual singles matches, which could well be in an equally complicated and delicately poised state. It has even been known ... wait for it ... for players to have a match against *their own partner* as well.

Did I mention that they quite like to bet at Sunningdale?

As I say, the whole gambling thing held no attraction for the other three but, if I'm honest, I did like to dip my toe in its murky waters every now and then. I also knew the punters a bit better than the boys did as I frequently played backgammon with them in the card room after playing. (Only after I'd turned eighteen, I should add. Cadets were not allowed into such a pleasure palace.) Indeed, for a number of years I led a golfing double life whereby I'd play my golf with Scotty and the two Marks, have a drink with them afterwards, then head up to the card room and play backgammon for hours with the punters.

And I have to say it was bloody fabulous. As any backgammon fan knows, the hours just whizz by and, as I was a half-decent player, I won more than I lost. (At least, that's how I remember it.) There was also something quite heady about the company in that room, housing as it did some fantastic golfers and senior members of the club. Gin rummy was their game of choice while the younger turks invariably stuck to backgammon.

If I'm honest, and as pathetic as it sounds, being there made me feel important. I was playing a game of chance for not inconsiderable stakes; I was being served drinks and food by waiters whom we would summon by phone; I was hob-nobbing with the members that mattered; and it was all taking place inside one of the most important, famous and influential golf clubs in the land. And of course, I was young and impressionable, so all of the above made my head spin.

But something wasn't right and it's only now, years later, that I can see what it was. Surely none of these people could really have been friends? Really, truly friends. And I don't just mean the guys I played with, but everyone in the room. Maybe I've got this wrong; maybe this is just how wealthy people behave, but the way I see it, if you can take large chunks of money off someone without batting an eyelid, then he can't really be your friend, can he? Sure, I laughed and joked with the guys I played with but I can't say we were interested in each other's lives. It was just get your drinks order in and down to business.

As I say, it could just be because I was the odd-one-out anyway, with one foot in both camps. Maybe some of the people there were indeed so wealthy that losing never hurt and winning never mattered. It sure wasn't like that for me. I was earning way less than my punter pals and when I lost, it bloody stung. I remember one weekday night taking my own board round to one guy's London flat, and four of us playing till the early hours. I lost £150 and I can still recall the nauseous despair I felt that night as I drove home.

Remember, this wasn't like a flutter at Ladbrokes. For the normal gambler it is bookmakers who are the enemy and no one feels the slightest compunction about taking Joe Coral to the cleaners. But this was different; these were people who you were going to play golf with the next day; who might be your partner in that game; who came round your house; who were 'friends'.

Right. So, what you're saying is, Mr Morals, that even if you could, you wouldn't do the backgammon thing again.

Are you kidding? Like a shot.

CHAPTER THREE: **PUTTING IS AN UNFATHOMABLE BUGGER: PART ONE**

(A) In my first ten years of golf I holed putts from all over the place, even though I was using an appalling putting stroke (hunched over the ball; all hands and wrists; looking up as I hit it). These days, I employ a classic textbook set-up and stroke, yet I can't hole a sausage. Answers on a postcard please, to the publisher's address at the beginning of the book.

(B) Unlike many professionals, I've never wanted to fall into that mental trap of thinking it's the putter that makes putts drop. It's a bit unseemly to see pro golfers, struggling with their putting, changing their putter after every round. They must know it's *their* fault; *their* faulty stroke; *their* mental block, and that even if they do stumble across a putter that goes round in 24, it'll only be a temporary respite. Over the years, I've used remarkably few putters – five, by my reckoning. This has got me nowhere. Arnold Palmer, on the other hand, has spent his whole life searching for the implement that will make him putt better; no design being too stupid. (Legend has it he has many hundreds of ridiculous clubs clogging up his garage.) One of us has won seven majors, the other The Arthur Lees Trophy.

(C) So much for doing the right thing.

CHAPTER FOUR: THE TEN MOST MARVELLOUS MOMENTS TO EVER HAPPEN ON A GOLF COURSE

There are too many golf stories. And not all of them are worth the telling.

The following are officially the ten best ever. They have been hand-picked and triple-distilled using only the finest ingredients. Every care has been taken to ensure that they reach you in perfect condition, as splendid as the day they occurred.

Mark Courage – Eighteenth hole, Sunningdale Old, One-Club Challenge Match

It was in the autumn, sometime in the late 1980s, and the drama was played out on the fearsome eighteenth hole of Sunningdale's Old Course, (448 yards uphill, bunkers everywhere, out-of-bounds by the green, snipers in the trees.) Every year, the weekend after my pals and I had been unluckily knocked out of the Founder's Singles, we would stage a One-Club Challenge on the Old, where we'd go round with a putter and one other club of our choice – usually a 4- or 5-iron.

Lowest score won, no strokes; the winner to keep for a year an original 1915 Braid Mills putter. ('Braid' as in James Braid of The Great Triumverate of golfers from the early nineteenth century, Braid, Vardon and J. H. Taylor – 'Mills' as in … no idea … for all I know, Mrs Mills, the chubby, jolly, knees-up piano player from the early 1960s.) I'd found the putter in my Dad's garage, yet it wasn't his and he had no clue where it had come from. It was a sign, by golly, so I promptly swiped it, and put it up as the prize in our One-Club Challenge.

As we stood on the eighteenth tee, the contest was all but over, with your correspondent being a full three strokes ahead of the boy Courage. It was mighty hard to make up three strokes on one hole and after I knocked my 5-iron up the fairway, Mark announced that, if no one objected, he was going to hit his drive with his putter.

We thought he was mad but, if he was game, we were too. With our arms folded and sporting an air of casual amusement, we watched as he smote the ball over 200 yards up the middle of the fairway with one of those classic Ping Ansers, as used by the world and his wife at the time. A bit low, to be sure, but dead straight and with a barrel-load of scampering top spin.

Seeing as how his tee-shot had been such a success, Mark figured he may as well play the rest of the hole with the putter; asking but one favour for his second shot – to tee the ball up on the fairway. While this would have been frowned upon by The Royal and Ancient it was perfectly fine with us, The Intrigued and Adolescent, so we stood back and let him hit away. Stone me, if he didn't knock the bugger over the cross bunkers and right onto the green … only to see it run through into a bunker back left. (Well, it is notoriously difficult to get a putter to check up from 220 yards out, after all.)

He holed the bunker shot.

A bunker shot that even Gary Player wouldn't have practised; with the pin cut really close to the sand, and on a sharp slope running away from the bunker. A shot that, even played with the right equipment, would be almost impossible to stop before the hole. A shot played with a club sporting only 1.5 degrees of loft and without the merest whiff of a flange.

He holed the bunker shot for a birdie.

A birdie 3 … up the eighteenth … with only a putter.

Playing it the only way possible, he had rapped it along the sand, run it up the face, popped it over the top, rolled it down the slope and nudged it into the flag with a clink and a plop. It was a moment of slack-jawed genius and well worth the slightly bent putter that he was now left with at the end of the hole.

I should add that I then three-putted for a six, putting us level on 83 shots each, and five minutes later had lost the extra hole and, indeed, the coveted Braid Mills putter. On reflection, it seems only right.

Hunter Phillips – Eighteenth green, Club Tournament Final

I don't care who you are, there isn't a golfer alive who hasn't stood over a short putt and felt a stone-cold certainty that they were going to miss it. Normally, one of only two things can then happen. You putt it and hole it, or, more likely, you putt it and miss.

There is a third possibility, though.

Hunter Phillips was an amateur, and one of the best

golfers at the Memphis (Tennessee) Country Club. In 1932 he was playing in the finals of the club tournament against Edward Falls. The match went to the last green where Phillips faced a three-foot putt to square the match and force extra holes.

He carefully studied the line from four different angles. Twice he settled over the ball, only to back away. Then, to the astonishment of everyone, he bent down, picked up the ball, and shook hands with his startled opponent.

'You got the match,' Phillips told Falls. 'There's no way I could make that thing.'

Ken Brown – First play-off hole, Sunningdale Old, 1986 European Open

Ken Brown, now an insightful and entertaining commentator, played for sixteen years on the European Tour, winning four times. He also won once in the States, and was a five time Ryder-Cupper. Much more interesting than what he did, however, is how he played the game.

Whippet-thin, he was not a golfer born to crush mighty drives. Instead, his talent lay in an instinctive feel for getting that little white ball into that little white hole, and an ignorance of what any instruction manual or teaching guru might have to say on the matter. His lanky, wiry frame would caress both chip and putt alike in a soft, squidgy, highly individual way, crouching so low to the ball you had to check twice that he was indeed using a club.

In contrast, by the time of the 1986 European Open at Sunningdale, Greg Norman was bestriding the golfing world like a colossus. He had won The Open in July for the second time, in the process becoming the first golfer to do so with four rounds in the 60s. If he could bag The European Open as well, he would also pocket a much publicised £50,000 bonus, on top of the winner's purse, to add to his rapidly swelling swag bag.

After seventy-two holes round Sunningdale's Old Course, however, and despite being 11 under par, victory was not yet his. Dash it if some feller by the name of Brown wasn't clinging on to his coat-tails and raining on his parade. They had tied on 269 and there was nothing for it but to set off down the par-five first hole in a sudden death play-off.

Twenty minutes later, one of them stood over a ten-foot putt to win the second most prestigious European tournament of the year.

Amazingly, it wasn't Norman, who had pushed his tee shot into trees, eventually scrambled an ugly par, and was now standing off to one side watching Brown putt for a birdie four and the biggest victory of his career.

As is always the case with play-offs, there were hundreds of people encircling the green, standing ten deep, as Brown prepared for the most important putt of his life. He prowled around for a bit … took a couple of practice strokes with his trusty hickory-shafted putter … settled over the ball … glanced once final time back at the hole … paused … and suddenly looked up at everyone.

'Hasn't it all gone quiet?' he said, to 500 incredulous ears.

There was a beat, possibly a beat and a half, and then everyone erupted into gasps of laughter, and strangled, half-caught yelps. Eyes bulged, jaws dropped, and hands were brought up to cover astonished mouths hanging open in the shape of the letter 'O'. Judging by Greg Norman's face, had he been drinking from a bottle of water, it would have been spat out in a spray of disbelief. The whole scene was an H. R. Bateman cartoon made flesh. Maybe, just maybe, you did this kind of thing if you won so often that a European Open was just another notch on your Adam's Tight Lies fairway 3-wood; or if you were the ever-joking Lee Trevino; or if you were asleep in bed having a dream; but not if you were Ken Brown.

Perhaps you've guessed what happened next. The spectators finally settled … he prowled around once more … took a couple of practice strokes … settled over the ball … glanced one final time back at the hole … paused … *and missed.*

The stupid, twatting, lovely bloke.

Sure enough, one hole later Norman was the champion; and while he's always been a player I've rooted for, this was a happy ending only for the Norman family and his friendly local Ferrari dealer.

No matter.

Ken Brown … walking 1-iron; 1986 Panasonic European Open Runner-up; and man with a delicious sense of the absurd … I salute you.

Walter Hagen – Eighteenth green, money match

Walter Hagen was not a shy man. If there was ever a golfer who had no need of a sports psychologist, it was Hagen. He knew, back in the 1920s and 1930s, what everyone is blathering on about today: that golf is all in the mind and that a positive mental attitude is worth a hundred buckets of balls.

What I love about Walter Hagen is that, by all accounts, he was a bit of a duffer. Every pro expects to hit bad shots, but normally, their idea of a bad shot is poles apart from yours and mine. (Don't you hate it when a Fred Funk, or a Steve Stricker plays their approach shot with a 3-iron, then turns away in disgust, only for cameras to reveal the ball dropping like a poached egg twenty feet from the pin.) Hagen regularly hit shots that would embarrass a rank beginner but, a bit like Ballesteros fifty years later, just saw these duffs as something that made the getting of a good score on that hole all the more interesting.

His swashbuckling brilliance was rewarded with plenty of trophies, both major and minor, and for the golf lover, he left behind a raft of priceless stories and quotes. For me, however, there is one less well known Hagen tale that absolutely takes the biscuit.

He arrived at a club one day to play a quiet game with friends. His impish nature got the better of him, however, and after he'd asked a member what the course record was, struck up a bet with him that, even though he'd never played it before, he would be setting a new course record that day.

Unsurprisingly, the member thought he'd have a bit of that, and soon word had spread and what seemed like half the club were placing bets here, there and everywhere. Hagen himself stood to pocket a tidy sum, as most people were betting against him.

When Hagen's fourball finally got underway they found themselves playing in front of a vast gallery, who stayed with them for his every shot. Wouldn't you know it, Hagen came to the last green still in with a shout. He had a fifteen foot putt for a birdie, a 66, a new course record, and a fair bit of dinner money.

The huge crowd shushed as Hagen settled over the putt. A couple of practice putts … a final glance at the cup … and then a firm rap sent the ball on its way.

At which point, Hagen, not even bothering to look at the ball and see what it was doing, looked up instead at the gallery and walked towards them with his hand held out.

It was still out, waiting for his money when, a few seconds later … inevitably … outrageously … the ball did Hagen's bidding, and fell into the cup.

Moe Norman – Exhibition match, Toronto, Canada

Moe Norman is, without a doubt, the greatest golfer you've never heard of. He could, literally, do anything he wanted with a golf ball. He had more control, more ability, and more belief than any golfer before, or since. (Including you-know-who.) So why have you never heard of him? Well, there's a story behind that. You can find out more about his extraordinary talent a bit later on but, for now, of all the astonishing things he did, the following is probably the coolest.

Norman is a Canadian and, for most of his career, played the Canadian tour (one reason why you've never heard of him). In 1969 Moe played an exhibition match with Sam Snead in Toronto. On one par-four a creek crossed the fairway, about 240 yards from the tee. Snead laid up just short of the water and, seeing that Norman had pulled out his driver, warned him that he wouldn't be able to clear the creek. 'I'm not trying to,' said Moe. 'I'm playing for the bridge.' To Snead's astonishment, and everyone else's, Norman's drive landed short of the creek, rolled across the bridge, and came out the other side.

Brian Barnes versus Jack Nicklaus −1975 Ryder Cup

He was a bit of a one, was Brian Barnes. The opposite side of the coin from the identikit, metronomic pro of today, he was a bull of a man whose frequently eccentric behaviour belied his seemingly effortless ability.

He would stroll round the golf course, pipe in mouth, with a certain air of detachment about him, as though he didn't really have anything else planned that afternoon so he might as well try his hand at some golf. The pipe would invariably stay clamped between his teeth as he hit his shots, and while they were still in the air he would stroll after them with an amused look on his face that would give no clue as to whether the shot was good or bad.

On the days that Barnes was on song, his unhurried, unconcerned manner made it look as though he, and he alone, possessed the secret of golf. It's always seemed surprising to me that he never won a major, but it probably doesn't bother Barnes much.

Uniquely, he had a penchant for playing in shorts. Khaki safari shorts if memory serves. And while Barnes' legs were not wholly unpleasant, large men and shorts tend not to go together and it must have required all his playing partners' powers of concentration to keep this rather startling image off their mental retina when playing their shots.

He liked a beer too. In fact, he liked six, which he would keep in his golf bag and suck on when the going got slow.

Once, he even marked his ball with a can of beer.

Oh, and there's one other thing.

He beat Jack Nicklaus in the Ryder Cup.

Twice.

In one day.

And this was in 1975 too, when the best golfer there's ever been was still as good as he ever was, having just won his fourth USPGA.

That year the Ryder Cup was being played at Laurel Valley in Pennsylvania and the Great Britain and Ireland team were getting their usual thumping when it came to the singles. (In those days, they played two singles matches on the last day.) In the morning, B. Barnes drew J. Nicklaus and to the amazement of all, promptly despatched him 4&2. 'I know how bloody mad he was, but he never showed it and congratulated me warmly,' Barnes recalls of his victory.

Indeed he was mad; so mad that he requested of captain Arnold Palmer that the draw be engineered so they could meet again in the afternoon. Bad move. He lost once more, this time 2&1.

Says Barnes: 'It gave the crowd something to watch and I remember Jack saying to me on the first tee; "You've beaten me once, but there ain't no way you're going to beat me again." And then he started – birdie, birdie – and I didn't think I would. But I did.'

So, just to get this straight … not only did Barnes beat Nicklaus twice in one day, but he did it in America, in front of a fiercely partisan crowd, and he won his afternoon match even though Jack Nicklaus … I repeat, Jack Nicklaus … was about as determined, and as focused, and as steely-eyed as he's ever been, about anything.

Honestly now … does it get any better than that?

Anonymous golfer – unknown course

The following is a story that I either read about, or someone told to me. If I read it, I can't remember where: if I was told it, I can't remember by whom. I have no idea of the name of the golfer, or where he played, or when all this was supposed to have happened. Indeed, it isn't even a 'moment' as such. All of which is thoroughly shoddy but no reason at all not to pass the story on.

There was once a man who decided he wanted to take up golf, so he bought some clubs and joined a nearby course. The problem was that his job was such that he could only play at extremely anti-social hours. Undeterred, he simply played by himself when the course was deserted. Happy with his own company, he quickly grew to love the game and played it whenever he could. If anything, as a complete beginner, he was quite glad he only ever played by himself, for he didn't like the idea of holding up more adept playing partners.

This went on for about a year until, quite suddenly, the man's circumstances changed and he found himself working the same hours as everyone else. For the first time he could play golf at a more civilised hour, so he went to his club, introduced himself to a few people, and fixed up a game. He wasn't too worried about letting himself down, for after a year of playing he was now a good deal more confident about his game and didn't think he would be too much of a liability.

He went round in level par.

His playing partners were amazed and they all told him what a wonderful player he was, and how incredible it was that he should play to such a standard having only just taken the game up. The man insisted however, that he was nothing special, and that he was just an average golfer. After all, he said, he had merely gone round in par. But par is a fantastic score, his new friends cried. The man was confused. But all I've done is what I'm meant to do, he said. The first hole is a par-four, is it not? They agreed that it was. And par is what you're supposed to do a hole in, is it not? Er … technically, yes, they agreed. Well then, he insisted, all I've done is what I'm supposed to do. Go round in par.

So the man's new friends sat him down and explained to him about golf; about how difficult a game it was, how frustrating and infuriating it could be, and how most golfers never even break 80.

Within six months, the man was playing off a 13 handicap.

Harry Vardon – 1920 US Open, Inverness Club

We're proud, occasionally to the point of smugness, that golf in Great Britain goes back such a long way. We rather like that our Open championship, for instance, began way before anyone else's. Shame then that we know so little about the great players of those early days.

Harry Vardon was the pick of the bunch, rising from humble beginnings to become the very best player in the world. He won six Opens, a total that seems more and more unbeatable with every passing year, and he was also the first overseas winner of the US Open.

And then there's the interlocking Vardon grip, adopted and popularised by the man himself over a century ago, and still used by … oh, pretty much every golfer in the world, really. (But not actually invented by him, fact fans – despite its name.)

He remained competitive well into his fifties, even after tuberculosis nearly killed him, and he almost won a second US Open in 1920 when he only failed to force a play-off by missing a three-foot putt on the seventy-second hole. Afterwards, a club member came up to him and asked how such a great player could miss such an easy putt.

Vardon decided there was only one way to answer such a question so he bet the man $100 (a monstrous sum in 1920) that one week from that day he could not sink exactly the same putt.

The bet was accepted.

The man, who was a low handicapper, spent the next week practising this one little putt and it's fair to say that after all that, he probably knew the line. Come the day the amateur stood over the three-foot putt in front of a huge crowd who had heard word of the wager. Just three measly feet stood between him winning (or losing) a small fortune.

Knees knocking, paralysed with nerves, he missed.

Robert Trent Jones Sr. – Tenth hole, Baltusrol

Robert Trent Jones was golf's most prolific architect, creating more than 350 courses on every continent except Antarctica. A small, cherub-faced man, his courses reflected his more sadistic side, festooned as they were with bunkers, ponds, creeks and vicious, undulating greens. Touring pros were not his biggest fans, but he couldn't have cared less, believing that he was merely defending par against the inexorable advance of technology.

'The shattering of par without a proper challenge is a fraud,' he often said. 'I make them make par.'

Before the 1954 US Open, Jones was asked to look at Baltusrol's Lower Course near Springfield, New Jersey. If it was going to host a US Open, the club wanted the course to be able defend itself and in such situations, who you gonna call? Jones set to work and, amongst many changes, redesigned the par-three tenth hole by adding a pond next to the green. Some members, however, felt the new pond was unfair and made the hole too hard, so Jones agreed to come and play the hole.

With him were the club pro and a couple of members, while many more members looked on. Playing from the 165-yard members' tee, his playing partners each knocked their ball onto the green. So far, the hole didn't appear to be too difficult. Jones then stepped up and swung a 4-iron. His ball landed on the green, rolled towards the cup, and fell in for a hole-in-one.

Turning to the members standing alongside the tee, he said: 'Gentlemen, the hole is fair. Eminently fair.'

And finally, the most marvellous moment of all:

Costantino Rocca – Eighteenth green, St Andrews, 1995 Open

You know what happened. I know what happened. Everyone knows what happened. Costantino Rocca fluffed his chip to the eighteenth, then holed a massive putt up and over the Valley Of Sin to force a play-off with John Daly, which he lost. Written like that, it doesn't seem like anything to get worked up about: someone played a bad shot, then they played a good one, happens all the time.

But hang on a nose-pickin' minute. How can Rocca's dramatic double-whammy be anything other than the most amazing, unlikely, astonishing, you-could-never-script-it moment in all of golf's rich history? Seriously, I challenge anyone to come up with a more incredible moment. It had everything:

It was to decide the tournament. If he chips and putts, it's a play-off; if he doesn't he comes second. It wasn't like it took place on the eleventh green on the second day, with plenty of holes coming after it – holes where anything could happen and anyone could still win. It was on the eighteenth, on the Sunday, and was the kind of pure, uncomplicated drama that only sport can throw up.

It was The Open. Not The Buick Invitational, or The Volvo PGA, or The Alphabetti Spaghetti Memorial. When golfers are practising their putting, they don't go, 'This for The Deutsche Bank Championship.' Winning The Open is the pinnacle achievement for any golfer. The reward for success is so astronomical, and the penalty for failure so terrible that, unless we have been there ourselves, we can have no concept of the pressure that Rocca was under. Interesting things happen all the time in golf, but for this to happen on the last green of the last day of The Open championship is what lifts it above them all.

It was at St Andrews. The home of golf and the venue that pros want to win at above all others. In the same way that a win at St Andrews is somehow more special, so too is an amazing moment.

It was two moments in one. The disaster of the fluffed chip, followed straight after by the outrageous putt. Hale Irwin sunk a forty-five-foot monster to get in the play-off at the 1990 US Open but, as marvellous as it was, it was just a putt. Had Rocca driven into the Valley of Sin and holed the putt from off the green for an improbable eagle and outright victory, that would quite possibly be the most incredible way anyone has won a major, but it still wouldn't top what he actually did.

It was a very, very, very long putt. Sixty-five feet, to be precise, which means it officially trounces Hale Irwin's snake as the longest putt ever holed to either win a major, or get into a play-off.

It was something that could have ruined his career, and the rest of his life. Had Rocca not redeemed himself with the putt, the consequences of his fluffed chip are simply too awful to contemplate. Doug Sanders has never shaken off his missed three-footer on the same green in 1970, and it would have dogged Rocca in the same way. It's one thing to have played a nervy chip to twenty feet and then missed the putt; as disappointed as you'd be, you could accept that. But to completely duff your shot, like a weekend golfer, in front of a TV audience of millions and millions, to blow your only chance of a major, surely that would gnaw away at your insides for ever?

Rocca himself is suspiciously blasé about his horror chip. 'On the eighteenth tee I said to my caddie that if I put it anywhere on the green I was going to hole it. Even on the chip I was convinced that I would hole it, but I tried to be too cute with it and duffed it. I was concentrating so hard that I had no idea what the fans were doing and my mind was so strong that the duff didn't affect me at all. When I looked at the putt I knew I would hole it. I just looked at the line, hit it and went to fetch my ball out of the hole. Maybe it was a bit lucky, as it wasn't a one-foot putt, but I really did think I would hole it.' It seems that the nice Mr Rocca would have us believe that hopelessly duffing the most important chip he had ever faced actually didn't faze him at all and that he took one look at the subsequent two-tiered, sloping, sixty-five foot putt for The Open Championship and knew he would hole it as not a single negative thought had entered his head. I particularly like: '*I just looked at the line, hit it and went to fetch my ball out of the hole.*' I'm not sure he's being entirely straight with us, but he has a lovely smile so, in the circumstances, I vote we let it go.

So there you have it: in everyone's eyes but his, the worst few seconds of Costantino Rocca's career, followed, just two minutes later, by the best. From utter, gutting despair to unconfined joy in 120 seconds. The moment to end all moments.

If you think you have a better one; an eye-popping tale that could knock Rocca into a cocked hat, I'd love to hear it. You're wrong … but I'd still love to hear it.

HONOURABLE MENTION, 'SPECIAL BONUS' MARVELLOUS MOMENT:

Trish Russell – Second hole, unknown golf club, Scotland

Yes, that's Trish Russell, wife of Richard Russell, the portly golfer and compiler of this very list. I know, it all sounds a bit fishy, but bear with me.

Trish and I were married in 1992 and for our honeymoon we drove around Scotland, seeing the sights, sniffing the smells, and staying in a different place every night. If this wasn't wonderful enough, Trish had also suggested that I chuck my clubs in the boot and maybe grab a game along the way. (No you can't have her, she's mine, and I've got the paperwork and everything.)

After a few days we happened to pass a nice little nine-hole par-three course, the name of which utterly escapes me. Next thing you know I've raided the boot, we've hired some ladies' clubs, and we're standing on the first tee.

The opening hole took a little while, but then, maybe I hadn't mentioned, Trish was a total beginner. This was the first time she had ever been on a golf course and the first time she had ever swung a golf club with intent. But hey, we were on honeymoon; in no hurry, and having a ball.

The second hole was around 150 yards, if memory serves, and Trish gave it a decent clonk, about half way up the hole. She then hit the same shot again and knocked it to the back of the green. The putt was forty feet, downhill, with a big swing from the right. I was just about to give her the old dustbin lid tip for long putts, when she went ahead and hit it anyway. It curled into the middle of the cup.

A par. On her second ever hole of golf; the first time she'd ever swung a club.

That's my missus, that is.

CHAPTER FIVE: PUTTING IS AN UNFATHOMABLE BUGGER: PART TWO

H e came into the locker room with the face of a man who had discovered how to turn porridge into gold. Only, this was even better than that. He had discovered The Secret of Putting. He was a Sunningdale member whose name I won't reveal, but whose heart was clearly in the right place as, considering the magnitude of his discovery, he was more than happy to share it with the world, without thought of personal gain. He could have taken his secret to Max Clifford, the impressively-haired PR guru, and made a mint. Books; magazines; DVDs; Putting School Academy in Miami; you name it. But no, he was happy to come into the locker room and share his good fortune with anyone in earshot who cared to have their game transformed.

His secret?

Cut across the ball with your putter.

Yup.

Slice your putts.

Apparently, this was guaranteed to send the ball in your chosen direction, and the cutty, out-to-inny action was perfect for producing a repeating stroke: the dream of every golfer.

Our man was quite serious about this, and got out his putter to show us all exactly how it worked. Someone gamely queried whether it might be a little unreliable, but Jeff Matey* was having none of it, and would just slice more putts across the locker room floor, all the while saying, 'Look' (putt), 'See?' (putt), 'See?' (putt), 'Look,' (putt).

And this is what putting can do. Forget its effect on your scorecard, that's just numbers; it's what it does to your head that needs addressing. Its insidious unfathomable-ness means that putting can actually turn your brain to mush. Like the game itself, it cannot be beaten, and only a loon would ever think he's got it licked. In this case it turned a perfectly normal, rational man into a wide-eyed, babbling fool whose grip on reason was no longer the Vardon one.

So please, ladies and gentlemen, it's only a game but I beg you ... let's be careful out there.

*While used here in a different sense, to keep a person anonymous, Jeff Matey was actually the name Mark Trickett and I would give to anyone whose name we didn't know, but needed to refer to. As in, 'Did you see Jeff Matey in the fourball behind us? Is he allowed to wear red trousers?' We've always thought the English language was a poorer, more incomplete, place without a phrase for this eventuality.

CHAPTER SIX: **THE READY BREK KID**

I know exactly how I'm going to be remembered as a golfer.

Sadly, it's not for my golf.

I could get three holes-in-one in a single round and it wouldn't make any difference. I could win the club Gold Medal with a 59 and it would not be my defining moment. I could triumph in the English Amateur, qualify for The Masters, make the halfway cut, come to the last needing only a five to win the tournament and make golfing history, putt into a bunker, take six, lose the play-off and fart loudly live on television in The Butler Cabin afterwards … and it would still not be the thing I was most remembered for.

For I am … The Man Who Never Wears A Sweater.

I don't wear one because I don't own one, and I don't own one because I get too hot if I play golf with more than one layer on.

It doesn't matter whether it's a bit nippy, bloody parky or so perishing cold that you get those white icicle eyebrows that mountaineers are so fond of. While everyone else sports sweaters, gloves, vests, waterproofs and fetching thermal pants, I'm striding around the course in a short-sleeve shirt looking, frankly, a bit stupid. I can't help it. I'm not trying to impress; I just don't get cold.

Well that's not strictly true. Standing on the first tee on a January morning, icy breath billowing, I'm as cold as anyone. But as soon as I start walking – literally, just twenty yards down the fairway – I warm up and become a perfectly comfortable body temperature. Should you shake my hand during the round – to congratulate me on a particularly fine shot, perhaps – it would be all lovely and toasty.

All this makes me an object of amusement and incredulity at Sunningdale and Rye and while the people I play with have got perfectly used to my appearance, it never fails to draw gasps from other members. I am like the weather: a constant about which everyone can comment. In the winter I stand out like Bob Hope's nose; in the summer, everyone remembers what I was wearing in the winter and jokes about how hot I must be now, and am I sure I don't want to take my shirt off.

Now, I am a fairly chunky bloke – fat, some might say – but it always seemed unlikely that my walrus-like blubber was the sole reason for my amazing heat retention. And so it proved when, a little while back, I had a cholesterol test done. Turns out my cholesterol level is abnormally low. So low, in fact that, to the astonishment of the nurse who took the test, my score didn't even register on the machine.

So there it was. No wonder I never get cold; my veins are like Shell pipelines; coursing blood round my body in an unstoppable, fur-free flow. I am a real-life Ready Brek kid with a warm orange glow emanating from my body, and a golf bag over my shoulder instead of a satchel. As a nice bonus, I'm also highly unlikely to have a heart attack; which just pips never having to wear a Pringle sweater.

Golf was always going to be my game. Right from the off, as I've said, I liked that you didn't have to wear shorts. My legs have never been my most fetching feature and, for the sake of others, taking up golf instead of the decathlon was the least I could do. It disturbs me that, thanks to Americans, shorts are creeping inexorably into the game but I am sustained in the knowledge that bare legs are hardly likely to become de rigeur at Sunningdale or Rye.

(One of my best pals visited Sunningdale once for a game with me and tipped up in some rather startling pin-striped shorts. Someone from the club immediately sidled up and firmly informed him that he couldn't wear them. And not because his socks weren't the right length: shorts were simply not tolerated at the club. Outwardly, I agreed with my friend that it was an absolute outrage and that golf clubs should just 'get with it'. Inside I was cheering like a bastard. Sorry Neil.)

I also liked the fact that golf was a sport where you didn't have to shower afterwards if you didn't want to. I know some people do but come on, it's just a leisurely stroll in the fresh air, for heaven's sake. At no point are sliding tackles involved and, while I have witnessed my fair share of violent swings, none would I deem so energetic as to merit a shower. You don't see people taking a shower after walking the dog, do you?

Maybe this means that golf isn't actually a 'sport'. I quite like the idea that a 'sport' is, by definition, an activity that requires a shower afterwards, and everything else is a 'game'. Thus, golf is a game; as is snooker; and bowls; and curling; and showjumping – but, amusingly, table tennis is a sport. (Have you played table tennis recently? My God, it's like a work-out in the gym. If every house had a table-tennis table we'd all be as fit as a fiddle.)

Anyway ... game, sport or sadistic mind-messer-upper, golf was my bag. In one way, at least, my golfing career has exactly mirrored that of Nick Faldo. For both of us there came a very definite point when we had to face up to the fact that we were a bit shit. Now, obviously, 'shit' in this case is relative. 'Shit' to Faldo was the realisation that he was only good enough to win the English Amateur, a handful of European Tour events, beat Jack Nicklaus in the Ryder Cup, and nearly win The Open. 'Shit' to Russell was a swing that was a blur, a fear of fairways, and a trophy cabinet that, over the course of a quarter of a century, had only ever been opened once.

The Arthur Lees Trophy 1984.

The only actual, honest-to-goodness, put-it-on-your-mantelpiece silverware that I have ever won. Sadly, it is the size of an egg cup and does not dominate a room in the way I'd hoped.

(The Arthur Lees in question was a blunt Yorkshireman who was the pro at Sunningdale for many years before I joined. As well as being virtually unbeatable over his home course – he would give even scratch players a hatful of shots, and still beat them – he had a reputation for speaking his mind. Once, so legend has it, he saw a tall, blond golfer on the practice ground and, as was his wont, he went and stood behind him, watching him swing. After a while he'd seen enough, muttering as he walked away, 'Ach, you've got no chance, laddie, no chance.'

It was Johnny Miller, just a few days before he won the Open at Birkdale.

Another time he saw a golfer in the practice bunker. Again, as was his wont, he went and stood behind him, watching him swing. After a while he'd seen enough and began telling the guy how he should be doing it. Peeved, the golfer said 'Look, I know how to get out of a bunker. I'll have you know that my father is Gary Player.' 'Ach, y'daft bugger,' said Arthur. 'Who'dya think taught yer father?')

While Faldo found Leadbetter, remodelled his swing, and went on to become the most successful British golfer ever (just ahead of Kenny Lynch), I found common sense, remodelled my swing as well, and fell in love with the game all over again.

It finally dawned on me, after twenty years of disappointment and anger, that hitting every shot like it was a long driving contest was perhaps not the right way to play golf. (In fact, it isn't even the right way to win a long driving contest.) At long last even I was beginning to see that taking a wedge from 160 yards out and hitting it as hard as I possibly could was not likely to result in the regular peppering of the flag. I have read some very eminent golfers advocate that encouraging youngsters to give the ball a merry whack is the best way to teach them. Let them hit the ball as hard as possible to start with, they say, and then straighten them up at a later date.

These people are terribly wrong and should be ignored like you would ignore a letter telling you on the envelope that you have already won a prize.

It turned me into a monster.

Between the ages of thirteen and thirty I was an angry young golfer. Which was strange, because away from the golf course I am a pretty optimistic, happy-go-lucky sort of bloke. Quite gormless, at times. It was only golf, with its limitless opportunities to fail and frustrate, that was my Achilles heel. Everything else I could take in my good-humoured stride, but golf brought out the sulky, sarky, snappy devil in me. Bashing the ball with all my might seemed to turn my mind violent as well as my body.

I remember having the most horrible games with my Dad during my first few years at Sunningdale. My natural golfing petulance joining forces with my natural teenage hormones to produce a silent, scowling misery-guts who would let one bad shot lead to a whole round of not trying. I would walk off greens and onto the next hole while Dad was still putting; I would barely speak to him all round; and. to cap it all, I would get annoyed that he wasn't getting annoyed at my appalling behaviour. My God, I'm amazed he ever played with me at all.

Playing all the time didn't help. It turned the game into something no more special or precious than my daily dump. Indeed, it would be wrong to call what I did a 'game' at all. It was a battle – me against the course; me against par; me against my inadequacies. I equated golfing enjoyment solely with scoring well, yet, and here's the rub, I wasn't a good enough golfer to score well. Despite this unarguable fact, I found it simply unacceptable to spoil a run of good holes with a double bogey, or hit a rank bad shot, or miss a tiddler. For some reason I really did think I should be going round in par or better, even though all the evidence suggested otherwise.

One day I did set a remarkable record though; one which may well have been equalled, but can never be beaten.

I walked in after one shot.

It was beautifully struck; straight over all the trees down the right of the first of the Old, and probably into the houses over the road, to boot. If I remember correctly my reasons for giving up were threefold. I was obviously going to play badly, so what was the point? I was obviously not going to shoot a new course record that day, so what was the point? I was a pathetic failure in everything I did or said, and life was just a series of crushing disappointments which made my very existence a hideous mistake that could never be put right, so what was the point?

My swing didn't help. It was hardly a thing of beauty and, while not ugly in a Jim Furyk way, was riddled with basic faults.

1. It was fast. Fast on the way back; fast on the way down; and with a pause at the top that was so infinitesimal that science was unable to actually measure it. My waggle was fast; my putting stroke was fast; and I positively wolfed down my sausage sandwich at the halfway hut. Every time I took the club back I embarked on a sequence of violent muscle movements over which I had no control. They say that the swing is a chain reaction and that if you start it correctly, everything cannot help but slot into place. The

reverse is also true. Start fast and you unleash a whirlwind that cannot be tempered, tamed or directed.

2. I over-swung (over-swang?) at the top and collapsed my hands as well, just for good measure. Now, over-swinging in itself isn't fatal – Tom Watson always went past the horizontal, John Daly takes it to insane degrees, and, as mentioned previously, my pal Scott was a dab hand – but couple it with floppy arms and it's like playing golf with a hosepipe. I had a video lesson once, and the swing sequence it captured shook me to the core. I remember going through the tape afterwards with Albert, the Scottish assistant pro, and him showing me, frame by frame, how much I was collapsing at the top. He paused it at the end of the collapse, with my club looking more like a back-scratcher, and said, 'Right, Richard, I'm sure you can see that this is an unacceptable position to be in at the end of your backswing. Now, let's have a look at your down-swing.' Trouble was, I hadn't finished. There were still two more freeze-frames where the club inched ever flatter.

3. Then there was my leg slide. An impressively flexible, but totally destructive move where shins, knees and thighs all thrust forward, and to the right, bringing the clubhead with it and blocking the ball out right. If I'm lucky it draws back onto the fairway or green. Failing that, the options are endless: it stays out right; it gets pushed even further right; it hooks; it duck hooks; and, on special occasions, it even slices, which when you're aiming right anyway, can prove spectacular.

I did other things wrong as well, but they were the big three. The ones that meant that any good shot was merely an accident. In combination, they also gave me my own, unique bad shot. The Russell Duff. A shot that I never saw anyone else ever hit, but one that I executed with shoulder-slumping regularity; especially off the tee. The swing that caused it never actually felt too bad, but the resultant hit would shoot off to the left, and scuffle along the ground until the rough finally ended its pathetic progress after thirty or forty miserable yards. I cannot tell you how dispiriting it was to stand on the first tee knowing that, regardless of the smoothness of my practice swing, or the virtue of my swing thoughts, I stood every chance of hitting my patented duff.

If I'd known any better, I'd have done something about it, but for all their handy hints on chipping, fairway woods and bunker play, I've yet to see the golf magazine that promises on its front cover '3 EASY STEPS TO CURING THAT 45 DEGREE SCUFF-SMOTHER'.

But one thing still confuses:

Why didn't any of the pros, during any of the lessons I had down the years, tell me to stop swinging like a fool? I mean, really tell me … in a way that would get through into my thick skull. I do remember doing something about my over-swing as a result of the video lesson, and I'm sure they sorted me out by the end of each session; got me propelling the ball vaguely straight and hitting it half decent, but I needed more than that. I didn't need advice that *made the best of what I had*, I needed a slap round the chops. Why didn't one of them ever ask me whether I wanted to be a real golfer? Was I happy just cobbling it round, or did I want to play good golf, that could win things, with a swing that would stand up to pressure? In short, what sort of golfer did I want to be?

Maybe I'm wrong to be blaming others. It was my swing; my responsibility; but what did I know? I was an immature, arrogant fool. I thought my swing was great. You couldn't hit a golf ball over 300 yards with a bad swing, surely?

The trouble with golf is that it needs discipline; you have to concentrate on every shot. It's not a reaction game, like tennis, or football, where you can slip into instinctive mode and let your body and mind make their own split-second decisions.

And this is where I come a cropper: I have no discipline. When I was in my twenties I was too hot-headed on the course to have any, and now that I'm older and wiser and playing much less, I'm having too good a time to have any. It's so bloody terrific to be out there that I want to enjoy every minute; the last thing I want is to furrow my brow and cocoon myself in 'the zone'. I want to have fun, stop to smell the flowers, and still play good golf. In short, I want to have my cake, eat it, and then lose weight as well.

It's not true, though, to say that I can *never* be disciplined. A few years back I discovered a sure-fire way of becoming a remorseless, machine-like golfer with the powers of concentration to rival a Formula One driver.

Unfortunately, I have to get angry.

Not the club-throwing kind of angry, but the sort that's directed somewhere else.

I was playing in a match for Sunningdale against Oxford University and my opponent in the morning game was a short, stocky, dark-haired student. He looked like the bastard son of a nightmarish liaison between Charles Bronson and Carla, the barmaid in *Cheers*. It was clear he fancied himself something rotten, and with good reason, for he played off 2 and hit one off the best drives I've ever seen off the first – arrow straight and with that glorious shape where the ball starts low and then curves upwards as it goes; like a Bobby Charlton net-buster. At the time I would have been playing off 7 or 8 and, as no strokes are given in these matches, I knew I was in for a tough old time.

As we set off it became clear that it would be tougher still as my poker-faced opponent made it quite plain that he didn't want to talk and just wanted to get on with the serious business of thrashing me out of sight. So far, so tiresome, but the clincher was that he had *brought his own caddy*: a middle-aged guy who was obviously a serious caddy and not just a bag-carrier. This was just a friendly little match between Sunningdale and Oxford; it wasn't The Ryder Cup, so what the hell was he up to?

Worse was to come.

We got to the first green and, if I'm honest, his various power plays were starting to have an effect. I wouldn't say I was beaten already, but I was certainly wondering how the hell I was going to get a result against this guy.

And then he holed his twenty-foot birdie putt. At which point his caddie punched the air with his fist and screamed, 'Yaaaaayyyyyy!!!'

Now hang on a second.

This was the last bloody straw.

In an instant my every thought became centred around wiping the self-satisfied grin off the faces of these two jokers. I promptly holed my own, only marginally shorter putt for a half, then slotted another twenty-footer to win the second, and a third long putt to win the third.

A couple of hours later I closed the match out on the fifteenth green and won 4&3, having played the fifteen holes in level par. I was so bloody determined to beat the little git, and in so doing deprive his unctuous caddie of a win bonus, that I simply forced myself to hit good shot after good shot. It was amazing. I felt no nerves, no trepidation, just a steely resolve over every shot. It was the most satisfying golfing performance of my life and while it was not an enjoyable game as such – not two words were exchanged between us for the whole round – it was certainly an extraordinary feeling to find myself so unerringly capable on a golf course.

Unsurprisingly, I have never been able to attain the same level of focus, and concentration, and determination to win, in any other round, be it strokeplay or matchplay. It will almost certainly, sadly, remain a glorious one-off.

Bugger.

I'm all depressed now.

CHAPTER SEVEN: **SEVE'S LAST STAND**

T he final day of the Ryder Cup will always throw up unlikely heroes. As sure as eggs is eggs, some unassuming journeyman will rise above their world-ranking and cement their place in history with golf they never knew they were capable of. Think Costantino Rocca beating Tiger Woods 4&2 in 1997. Think Peter Baker at the Belfry in 1993. Philip Price and his Mickelson-mashing heroics in 2002. And, of course, Philip Walton in the 1995 Ryder Cup – the one staged in America at Oak Hill, and won by Bernard Gallacher's underdog European side, courtesy of Walton's last-hole, last-gasp victory against Jay Haas.

The one European that no-one would nominate as a hero that day is Severiano Ballesteros. Shoved out first because he was playing so atrociously, Tom Lehman beat him 4 and 3 and got the Americans off to a sadly predictable fast start that so nearly ended in victory. All week Seve had been a shadow of his former, all-conquering self and, if we're honest, the 1995 Ryder Cup is the one that we tend to conveniently forget when it comes to assessing Ballesteros's unbelievable record in the event. Under-standably, it's the one match we gloss over, so as not to tarnish the reputation of the greatest Ryder Cupper ever. After everything he's done for us, we owe him that, surely?

Well, a funny thing happened on the way to winning the Ryder

Cup that year. Turns out Walton wasn't the only lowly-ranked European to perform great deeds that Sunday. Turns out Seve played one of the most remarkable matches in Ryder Cup history.

It's just that no one knows.

Somehow, his exploits that day slipped right under the radar. Perhaps, out of politeness and respect, people didn't really pay attention to his match against Lehman. After all, there was plenty of stirring stuff going on elsewhere, why witness the painful last rites of a legend? Whatever the reason, the real story behind Seve's seemingly straightforward defeat has rarely surfaced.

So, in tribute to the most gifted and charismatic European golfer these shores have ever seen, it's time to set the record straight.

It was early morning on the last day of the Ryder Cup. Severiano Ballesteros, the superhuman force at the heart of the European side, had slept badly and was up with the dewsweepers, hitting balls on the range long before the crowds had gathered. Normally such an unstoppable mass of confidence and will, he was, for once, anything but. The great man was anxious. Anxious about his match against Tom Lehman; anxious not to let his team-mates down; anxious to find a swing – any swing – that could keep him on the short stuff and out of the ten billion trees that seemed to pepper the course. And frankly, he had every right to be anxious. His game was coming apart at the seams and there wasn't a damn thing he could do about it.

It's debatable whether his practice that cold autumn morning in upstate New York did him any good at all; his shots going left, right and, only very, very occasionally, centre. The irony being that, as ever with Seve, his swing still looked pretty good to the untutored eye. Had you stood in front of him, and not behind, you could even imagine you were still watching the Seve of old. But as anyone who had seen him play the preceding two days would testify, the truth was that Seve simply had no idea where he was going to hit the ball. We all have those days; we all have those practice sessions; but not all of us then have to walk to the first tee and play the opening match in the Ryder Cup singles.

Amazingly, he had actually won his foursomes with David Gilford the previous day. Through a combination of Seve's still astonishing short game, and his ability to make whoever was partnering him feel like they were the best player in the world, he and the under-rated Gilford had despatched their opponents. But now he was on his own, and no amount of smouldering, steely-eyed grit could save him.

The theory was to put Seve out first where his loss would be least harmful to the team; a far cry from previous years where the mighty Spaniard would demand to be unleashed first because, like some snapping, snarling attack dog, he simply couldn't wait any longer before descending on his prey. But while others may have seen Seve's position at the head of the matches as a damage limitation exercise, the fiercely proud Spaniard saw things differently. He saw it as a chance to lead his troops; a chance to defy the odds (something he had relished doing all his career – like being the first European golfer to conquer America) and inspire those that followed him.

When he arrived on the first tee Lehman was already

there, laughing and joking with Loren Roberts. Seve nodded an acknowledgement and no more. He'd never been big on hand-shaking and chit-chat, and wouldn't be starting today.

'Ladies and gentlemen. Welcome to the first singles match between Seve Ballesteros (the crowd cheered) and Tom Lehman (the crowd roared).'

The excited spectators slowly settled. Eventually, they fell into a respectful, but unreal, silence.

'First on the tee, Seve Ballesteros.' More cheers as Seve stepped forward. He mouthed a couple of thank-you's, swung a couple of good-looking practice swings and, as the crowd quietened once more, addressed the ball. Two accusatory glances down the fairway, and then he hit it.

The ball went so far left it drew a gasp of surprise from the crowd. It flew dead straight into thick trees and left everyone whispering and chattering about what they had just witnessed. They knew Seve was playing badly but to see a professional golfer hit a shot so far off line was both shocking and thrilling.

Lehman found the fairway and then found the green, while Seve found his ball, but in an unplayable lie – even for Seve – leaving him no option but to drop it and advance his third up towards the green. Seve sees shots around the green the way the rest of the world sees putts, so it was no surprise to see his chip for par threaten the flag, but finally finish eight inches short. Lehman duly knocked his birdie putt to three inches. Hole won. But not quite; for there was a long pause before Seve actually conceded the putt. Even though Lehman had braced himself beforehand (at the urging of his fellow Americans) to ignore any mental game-playing from Ballesteros, this seemed to throw the American a bit. He knew that Seve had a reputation for using every trick in the book to gain an edge, but surely he hadn't seriously considered asking him to hole a three-inch putt?

Still, 1 up to the USA.

The second hole unfolded in similar fashion to the first, with one big difference. Seve's drive was as far right as his first drive had been left. He found himself in thick rough but still managed to dig out, in the circumstances, a terrific second shot that curled round a tree and up towards a greenside bunker. Lehman played the hole well, and stopped his approach shot on a sixpence just eight feet right of the hole. Sensing blood – and even at this stage of the match, thinking thoughts of the first American point – the crowd roared with delight.

Despite Seve's cleverly manufactured recovery shot, he was still in light rough, facing an awkward and delicate little pitch over a bunker, with precious little green to work with. He measured up the shot, seeing it in his head and feeling it in his hands and arms and shoulders. A couple of crisp practice strokes and the ball was airborne, landing softly at the green's edge and rolling up the hill.

Four seconds later, it rolled right into the hole.

The huge roar that followed it must have been like oxygen to Seve. Prince Andrew happened to be beside the green and, in his joy, slapped a complete stranger on the back. In the commentary box, Paul Azinger said nothing, but looked horrified. Tom Lehman, hangdog at the best of times, looked like he was going to be sick.

Ballesteros had birdied a hole he had never been out of

trouble on.

Quickly recovering his composure, Azinger spoke quietly over the scene. 'This reminds me so much of The Belfry in '93,' he intoned. 'At the team dinner Chip Beck stood up and told us that sometimes the will to win can overcome a mechanical breakdown. Seve is overcoming a mechanical breakdown.'

Lehman still had only eight feet for a half but, as if pre-ordained, it slid by the hole. We were only on the second hole; he wasn't losing, but Lehman couldn't have looked sicker. The match was all square, yet Seve hadn't found a single fairway, or green, in regulation, while his opponent hadn't missed either, on either hole. On top of which, Seve had that look in his eye; you know the one … that Ryder Cup look. He charged off to the next tee.

The third hole was a par-three and, no doubt to everyone's disappointment, was halved with two straightforward pars – both players hitting the green and two-putting from some way away.

The fourth hole was a long par-five which promised a return to the high-jinks of old, and didn't disappoint. Seve was up first and, as he prepared to hit, you couldn't help but notice how the crowd lining the fairway were looking back more cautiously than normal, ready to duck on the 'F' of 'Fore'. Seve hurled himself into the shot and, sure enough, the cry went up. Everyone covered their heads and waited for the clattering of ball on branches … which never came. Indeed, no one seemed to have a clue where Seve's ball had gone. There was much searching around when word finally reached the crowd that Seve's ball had in fact hit a tree full on and rebounded back towards him, finishing up in ugly-looking rough only a few feet in front of the tee. A drive that had only gone twenty yards – that was a first, even for Ballesteros.

Luckily for Seve, Lehman's drive sliced wildly into trees on the other side of the fairway.

No, you're right. That didn't happen.

Lehman split the fairway once more. Then Seve bludgeoned his ball out, only to see it go into more rough down the right hand side. Then came possibly his most extraordinary shot of the day – a 3-wood from out of the crap that soared on and on and on, till it actually landed on the front of the green, some 240 yards away.

On the face of it, shots like Seve's 3-wood that day defy all logic and make a mockery of his inability to hit his drives onto the fairway. How can a man hit his drives – off a tee remember – at an angle of forty-five degrees, but then hit an infinitely harder 3-wood from out of the rough straight enough to hit the green? Well … maybe Seve can only see his shots if they have to be conjured up; manufactured; created by his imagination? Maybe a tee-shot is simply too easy; the fairway too wide. (When was the last time you applauded and cheered a fairway hit?) Where's the glory in landing on a strip of land 80 yards across? Anyone can do it. Why would genius bother itself with something as mundane as a tee-shot? As we speak, who's the number one in the stats list for fairways hit? I'll tell you. Fred Funk. Exactly.

After Seve's heroic finding of the green, there then followed a lovely moment when the radio operator at the side of the green was unable to persuade his boss back in the press tent that both Lehman *and* Ballesteros were putting for birdie. 'What are you talking about?' said the man, angry at being mucked about. 'You just told me Seve's drive only just got off the tee!'

Both players then two-putted for par, though what the scorecard doesn't say is how Lehman's birdie putt, when just a foot from the hole, looked for all the world as though it was going to drop, only for it to lip round the edge. Lehman sank to his knees in frustration and despair. In hindsight, one can't help thinking that Lehman's agonised histrionics could only have added to his already agitated state and, in turn, given succour to Seve, who of course likes nothing better than to see his opponents squirm.

So, that's the last two holes halved … somehow … and the match still level.

On to the fifth. Where Seve hit a tee-shot that surpassed anything he had hit before. There is a stream that runs along the right-hand side of the fifth and is designed to punish the seriously off-line. Ballesteros's ball cleared it with ease and finished in a meadow which had probably never been visited by a golf ball before. Seve's relief at avoiding any serious trouble was somewhat punctured though, when he reached his ball. There was a huge tree that towered in front of him which was directly between him and the green. To the few who could see, it didn't seem possible that he could get his ball up quickly enough to clear it. Seve thought otherwise, but despite its steepness, chose not to take on the shot with a sand wedge, or a wedge, but a 9-iron. Not content with just clearing the tree,

Seve had his sights on the green as well.

The shot he proceeded to hit defied belief. Never had a 9-iron been hit so vertically, yet covered such a distance; never had Pythagoras had his mathematical theorems so roundly disabused. (There was talk of the club commemo-rating the shot by putting a plaque where he had struck it. It's probably a good job it never happened; who would ever pass by there to see it?) Sure enough, the ball cleared the tree, to be followed a few seconds later by an almighty roar as it also found the green, albeit right at the front, sixty feet from the cup. There was a definite sense that, no matter what their nationality, the crowd were getting behind the Spaniard now, unable to resist his miraculous shot-making and buccaneering spirit.

As it happens, as marvellously as he had done, the putt he had left himself was such a tricky one that Seve couldn't get it closer than ten feet. Lehman, meanwhile, had once again knocked a beautiful second to eight feet, so it was still Seve's turn to putt.

This meant we had Seve putting for a par-four, and Lehman putting from closer in for a birdie three. As if you hadn't already guessed, Seve holed and Lehman missed: the American's putt also lipping out again, just for good meas-ure. And still we weren't finished – Lehman looked over at Seve for confirmation that the twelve-incher he had left was given, only to see Seve doing what Seve always does beside the green; practising his putting stroke with his eyes firmly downward, to the exclusion of all else. Getting the message, Lehman duly holed his putt for a half. Match still level.

There had already been a European hole-in-one at the

short sixth, courtesy of Costantino Rocca, and with Seve's flair for drama no one would have been surprised if Ballesteros had got another one now. It didn't happen; instead Seve left his tee-shot way short in deep rough, while Lehman struck a wonderful 6-iron to seven feet. Seve dug out his chip to five feet then, once again, saw his opponent miss his birdie putt. At least it didn't lip out this time. Inevitably, Seve holed his tricky putt for a half.

As he left the green, Seve glanced at the scoreboard to see that, of the matches behind, Mark James and Jacobson were each 1 up and all the rest were level.

On to the seventh, and Seve (still with the honour, which must have added insult to injury to Lehman) blasted it dead right towards the one part of the hole you didn't want to go – the watery and the tree-y part. He evaded the water but, instead, left himself behind a willow tree. Lehman drove another beauty down the middle of the fairway. Indeed, you have to hand it to Lehman; he may have been in the middle of the most surreal and frustrating match of his life, but his golf remained sublime. It would have been the easiest thing in the world to let Seve's amazing escapology act put doubt in your head and kinks in your swing, but as determined as Seve was, Lehman was concentrating every bit as hard.

Mind you, that didn't mean he was having a good time. As he walked slowly and reflectively up the fairway, an American spectator shouted: 'Don't worry, Tom, he can't keep this up.' Lehman's face said that he wasn't so sure.

Seve successfully bent his second round the offending willow tree, and then pitched to ten feet above the hole.

Lehman hit yet another great approach shot, this time leaving his ball twelve feet away. Lehman then struck another good putt, this time just missing on the left. Seve then holed another brilliant putt for a half, this time a perilously quick downhill twister. As he strode purposefully to the next tee, he didn't just have the momentum with him; he had what seemed like most of the crowd as well. Everyone seemed to be shouting: 'Go, Seve!' There was no urgency to check out what was happening to the rest of the matches – everyone realised that they were witnessing something unique in the history of this great event. The facts were extraordinary. Seve had missed every fairway – but not just missed them as you or I might: he hadn't come within thirty feet of finding the short grass. Meanwhile, Lehman had found every fairway – indeed the centre of every fairway – and had peppered the flag with almost all of his approaches. Yet they were still level. Could Seve achieve the impossible and actually go on to win this match? How much more could Lehman take without cracking?

Well, the history books record that the pendulum began to swing at the next: the eighth. Seve left himself a chip-in for his par, and almost pulled it off, sinking to the ground in pain as the ball just tickled the side of the hole. Seeing as Lehman had two putts from six feet to win, Seve reluctantly conceded Lehman the hole, though not before the American had had to line it up and mentally prepare to play it.

The ninth broke the pattern slightly. Lehman actually missed his first fairway, and Seve, unable to capitalise, missed his seventh out of seven. The hole was halved.

At the tenth something miraculous happened. Ballesteros hit his drive onto the fairway, accompanied by a huge cheer. (My theory is that he didn't bother using a tee peg, and placed the ball in a divot instead; impossible shots being the only ones he could actually hit straight.) But sure enough, playing his approach from perfectly manicured grass proved far too easy to do properly and, to the groans of the watching Europeans, he dumped his second in a greenside bunker. From then on, however, the hole played itself out according to the script. Lehman hit his closest approach of the day (to four feet), Seve sank a curly six-footer for par, and Lehman missed his putt to win the hole – this time seeing the ball horseshoe out and actually come back towards him.

Hole halved. Lehman still just 1 up.

Seve needed the par-three, 192-yard eleventh to be a much harder shot than it was, offering up as it did the largest green on the course. He missed it on the right and, for once, was unable to get down in two. Lehman scored a regulation par and that was that. Two down.

Just as Seve was about to tee off on the twelfth there was a huge cheer from the green they had just left, and Seve was forced to step back and wait for the hubbub to die down. Howard Clark had just got a hole-in-one. For the first time in two hours of combat, it dawned on everyone that there were other matches on the course.

A rare thing happened on the par-four twelfth – both Lehman and Ballesteros reached the green in the regulation two shots. As they walked up the fairway, it was fascinating to watch the body language of the two men. Had you arrived on the course at that moment and played 'Spot The

One Who's 2 Up' you would have lost your money. Seve was striding purposefully toward the green, eyes blazing, anxious to play the next shot, while Lehman was trudging along behind, clearly drained.

It was Lehman to putt first and he left it six inches from the hole on the line of Seve's putt. He looked at Seve, more in hope than expectation, and asked whether the putt was all right. 'Mark it,' was all Seve said. But instead of doing so, Lehman tapped it in.

Seve pounced. 'What are you doing? You play out of turn. Where is the referee?'

'I honestly thought he was going to claim the hole, there and then,' Lehman was to say after the match was over.

Seve's reaction caused an immediate change in the crowd, who had been on his side up until now. They began to boo and jeer and told him to play on. The thing was, he was totally within his rights to ask a referee to replace Lehman's ball, which, when the referee arrived, it duly was.

'I wanted to use his marker as a line for my putt,' Seve said afterwards. 'Of course I was going to give him the putt; it was very close.'

Whatever the rights and wrongs, the result was that it made Lehman angry. He felt that Seve was pushing the boundaries of sportsmanship, and he had just about had enough.

(It gets confusing here. It seems rather odd that Lehman should think that Seve was seriously out of order, because the accusation just doesn't stack up. Pros frequently use someone else's ball marker as a marker for their putt, if it happens to be positioned on the green in the right place. The crowd might not know that it's a common practice, but Lehman should have; and don't forget, Lehman tapped his putt in *after* Seve had asked him to mark it. If he'd just marked it as requested – which Seve was perfectly entitled to ask him to, and goes on all the time in matchplay golf, *no matter how small the putt* – the ensuing brou-ha-ha would never have happened, and Lehman would never have got angry; an emotion which dispels negative thoughts and serves only to make people more determined. But for that, Seve could well have continued to put pressure on an increasingly worried opponent and changed the outcome of the match.)

After all that, Seve missed the putt and the hole was halved, leaving Lehman still 2 up. As it turned out, that was probably the defining moment of the match for, only minutes after Seve had failed to bring it back to just one hole between them, Lehman made a straightforward par at the next for a win, and took the match to 3 up. As he holed his shortish putt, Lehman punched the air and milked the applause of the crowd. He was a different man now they were back on his side again.

At the fourteenth, Lehman sank his only sizeable putt of the whole match – a twenty-footer for birdie – and launched into an even more showy celebration. He was now 4 up with four to play but, more importantly, the momentum was with him and even though Seve could chase a lost cause like no man before or since, there was no way Lehman was going to let it slide now. He even caught Seve's eye and gave him a less than friendly glare.

Lanny Wadkins, the captain of the American team, hot-footed it over to the short fifteenth to be present at the winning of his side's first point. It followed soon after when Seve's chip from the back of the green just missed the flag. Suddenly, it was over, and the two men were shaking hands. Seve was very animated and seemed to be trying to explain what happened on the twelfth. Lehman was crying and nodding and slapping him on the back. The green was then invaded by a media scrum.

'That was the toughest guy I've ever played,' said Lehman. 'He was absolutely unbelievable. I salute him. He didn't deserve to be booed at the twelfth, and he was perfectly within his rights to ask for my ball to be replaced. He is a real gentleman.'

Ballesteros too was talking to reporters: 'It was a great match. The twelfth was bad. The crowd didn't understand. They thought we were going to have a fight. He's a heavyweight; I'm a lightweight. I wasn't claiming the hole. I wouldn't want to win the hole that way.'

Much later, Seve elaborated on his amazing match. 'Today was the hardest fight I have ever had with my driving. I knew it would be a tough day, with the way I was playing and the way the course is. Who knows, maybe if I had not bogeyed the eleventh, Lehman would have cracked and I would have won.'

Who knows, indeed? With everything that was happening to him, Lehman had been even tougher than Seve not to let his despair turn itself into bad shots. It was only once he got the bit between his teeth that he pulled away, and if fate hadn't thrown up the incident on the twelfth, maybe Seve could indeed have broken him.

But although he hadn't won, Ballesteros had done the one thing he wanted to do. He had hung in there and shown the way to his team-mates. He had, against all the odds, lead from the front. All the while he was no worse than 1 down, there was a chance, a tiny, slim, sliver of a chance, that he could provide his team with the unlikeliest of points. As long as he was in with a shout, he was an inspiration to those who followed.

A few hours after Seve's match ended, Phillip Walton stood amidst unbearable tension on Oak Hill's eighteenth green, encircled by a vast throng. With a slow, small swing of his broomhandle putter, he kept his nerve, cosied the ball to the hole side, and the Europeans had won on America soil for only the second time.

Severiano Ballesteros had also played his last Ryder Cup as a golfer. And while it no doubt peeves him that his final match ended in defeat, those who saw it are in no doubt.

It was, very possibly, his finest hour.

CHAPTER EIGHT: PUTTING IS AN UNFATHOMABLE BUGGER: PART THREE

Why do golf commentators think that a straight, uphill putt is the easiest putt you can get?

Can't they see? Are they blind? It's the hardest, for heaven's sake.

In order to hole a ten-foot, straight, uphill putt you have to do everything right; you have to hit the perfect putt. Any flaw in your stroke and the ball will not … *not* … go in. If you do not hit it straight, on line, and at the hole, it will not go in. (How can it? There's no borrow to bring it back.) If you do not make a firm, positive stroke at the ball, it will not go in. (How can it? It's uphill; it won't get there.)

This is not true for other putts. We've all holed putts that we didn't think would get there; you just have to be mistaken in how slow you thought the green was. We've all holed putts that we have under-borrowed, or over-borrowed; all you have to do is get the line wrong to start with. It's one of the few things about putting not designed to turn you into Herbert Lom from the Pink Panther films: you can hit crappy putts that still manage to go in.

Just not, ever, when standing over a ten-foot, straight, uphill putt – the hardest putt you can ever face, no matter what the so-called experts say.

CHAPTER NINE: PUTTING IS AN UNFATHOMABLE BUGGER: PART FOUR

W hy do golf commentators think that a fast, downhill putt is the most difficult putt you can get?

Don't they understand? To someone with a fearful, uncertain stroke (that'll just be eighty per cent of the golfers on the planet), they're the best putt you can ever have. My heart leaps when I see that I've left myself a vicious downhill slider. My confidence grows and the levels of positive energy I give off would shame Sting himself.

Why? Because a downhill putt only needs to be sent on its way; just given an encouraging little nudge, like a chick from the edge of a nest. It doesn't need a firm, positive stroke with a classic, extended follow-through, it just needs a teeny, tiny little tap that gets the ball rolling; the green then does the rest. You can lift your head too early; you can jab at it; you can be all wrists; you can stand on one leg, hold the putter with one hand, and sing 'Chirpy Chirpy Cheep Cheep': none of this matters when your putter head only moves an inch back, and an inch forward. How can it?

Plus … and here's the kicker … you're expected to miss. The pressure's off. In fact, you'll be clapped on the back if you just avoid three-putting. You can't lose.

No, I'm sorry, God bless the downhill slider – the easiest

putt you can ever face, no matter what the so-called experts say.

Unless, of course, you knock it ten feet past.

In which case, see previous chapter.

CHAPTER TEN: **THE HALFWAY HUT**

S o here we are, roughly halfway through the book. How about we stop for five minutes and grab a bite to eat and a quick slurp of something?

I very much like the idea of the halfway hut. After nine or so holes of honest endeavour, how civilised it is to sit for a few minutes and ruminate on the topics of the day with a sugary tea/milky coffee/orange squash to hand. It says something good about a game, I feel, when its combatants can stop halfway through, not for physical rest, but for flap-jacks and Bovril. Incredibly, some people don't care for it and prefer to march ahead to the next tee and continue their grim-faced progress. Perhaps they're playing so badly they just want the round to be over as soon as possible. Per-haps they are rushing to keep an appointment. Perhaps they are just joyless curmudgeons. Whatever, the names and faces of these people should be sought out and mentally filed. That way, not only will you never have to play with them, but in the event that they ever ask you for your daughter's hand in marriage, you will be ready for an instant rebuff.

The halfway hut at Sunningdale is a grand example of its kind, and is one of two reasons why the tenth on the Old is such an uplifting hole. Standing on the tee you face a gasp-inducing view as the hole plunges down the side of a hill and stretches into the distance. Not only does this make you feel like you could very well launch the longest drive of your life, but there, way, way in the distance, nestling by the side of the green, is a chunky, but unpretentious little hut. An oasis of food and drink.

There has been a refreshment stop by the tenth green ever since the earliest days of the club, around the turn of the century. In the beginning it was just a man under the trees, known as 'The Gingerbread Man', selling arrowroot biscuits and ginger beer, but these days it's an altogether more thorough affair. The ever-smiling Vernon has been refreshing the peckish and the parched there for eight years now, assisted by his equally cheery cohorts, Derek, Ruth, Gwen and Dawn. Together, they proffer up all manner of drinks and an astonishing array of foodstuffs, from delicious hut-made sandwiches, to fancy cakes, to boiled eggs, to confectionery of every kind, to their signature dish – the sausage – either in a sandwich, or not.

They also make a unique vegetable soup for the winter months whose exact recipe, much like that of Coca-Cola, is known only by a select few who, for safety reasons, are not allowed to travel together or watch, as a group, any of the films of Michael Winner. In itself, their soup is delicious (and I don't even like vegetable soup) but, for the adventurous diner, it is also served another way. You can, if you wish, ask for 'soup with'. What you get is the same glorious stuff, but with a healthy splash of sherry in it, which gives the dish an added *je ne sais quoi.* (Why the 'soup with'? Because at one point the hut didn't have a licence to serve alcohol, so a codeword was deemed necessary.)

Sunningdale's special bangers remain the star attraction, however, and they average around 1200 sausages a week. One customer is particularly partial. As Vernon puts it, 'We have an order of merit for sausage eating and in the lead, and almost untouchable, is Ulster professional Darren Clarke, who has been known on occasion to gobble down seven during his brief visit.'

Untouchable, eh Vernon? That, sir, is fighting talk, and I've a good mind to make an official bid for a new record at my next visit. Darren Clarke is a lovely guy and a fine golfer, but sausage-eating at the hut is an amateur sport with a proud history, and I consider it my duty to club and country to bring the record back home to the common man. Watch this space.

Right then, have we finished? Then let's carry on. Your honour, I believe.

CHAPTER ELEVEN: IS IT A BIRD? IT IS A HELICOPTER? NO, IT'S A SIXTY DEGREE LOB WEDGE

For a number of years, club-throwing was a speciality of mine and a game at which my handicap was plus-2. Say what you like about the rights and wrongs of club-throwing, it is an immensely satisfying thing to do. If I close my eyes I can still hear the 'whump, whump, whump' of a misbehaving 4-iron as it's despatched into the far yonder.

As a spear-chucking youngster, I was always amazed that more people didn't throw clubs. Golf is, without doubt, the most maddening game to play, yet everyone who did so was expected to bottle up their emotions and spend four hours as though on medication. Don't get me wrong, I loved that golf was a more civilised game than all the others. That was its appeal. I was all in favour of etiquette, and decorum, and dress codes, and respectful silence when others were hitting, and lifetime bans for anyone caught marking their ball two inches closer on a twenty-foot putt. Golf made all other sports seem like a charter for cheats and bullies. Golf was undoubtedly the last bastion of decency and sportsmanship. It was even in the rules that if you were better than your opponent, you had to give him extra shots till he stood just as much chance of beating you. How gloriously bonkers and sporting was that?

I just couldn't understand why you weren't allowed to get annoyed.

Golf is so blinkin' difficult, and offers so many opportunities to fail, why was it so wrong to react spontaneously, and honestly, to its most galling moments? Surely, if you didn't react, you couldn't care, and what could be worse than playing a sport without passion? No matter how wonderful a game it may be, the truth is that disappointment and frustration lurk along every yard of a golf course. Exasperation is a golfer's constant companion; and it doesn't matter who the golfer is, or how good they are. (Ben Hogan himself is quoted as saying that he only expected to hit two shots 'properly' all round.)

Looking back, the bit that I regret is not the actual chucking, but the petulant sulk that would invariably follow it. Watching someone hurl a club is funny. Watching them spend the next two or three holes saying nothing, not trying, and walking really, really, *really* slowly must be hugely tiresome.

By my mid-twenties it had reached a point where club-throwing had became just another aspect of golf – no different to bunker play or reading greens – and when you 'threw' as often as I did you couldn't help but become interested in the science of club propulsion.

Basically, club-throwing is not as easy as it looks, and while I can, of course, now see that hurling your equipment about in a huff is perhaps not the most considerate way to behave on a golf course, I feel it is still my duty to pass on what I learnt about trajectory and technique for today's generation of moody club-slingers.

The Whirler

Not all club-throws go 'whump, whump, whump'. That
only happens if you're a 'Whirler', and heave the club
round from the side of your body, thereby promoting a
spinning and twirling flight. The most natural, instinctive
throw of all, 'The Whirler' was my chuck of choice as it
was a wilder, more out of control throw that better served
the animalistic release of pent-up anger. It was also a very
hard throw to direct as it tended to go way to the left of
where you were aiming; the in-to-out swing encouraging a
pull-hook. I liked this. The fact that I couldn't send an
object in the direction I wanted it to go was what had got
me into this state in the first place. The last thing I needed
now was to execute a perfectly controlled and accurate
club-throw; it wouldn't have been in keeping with the
spirit of the moment.

The Hammer

For those whose rage was of a more simmering, 'oh, for
heaven's sake' nature, 'The Hammer' was the perfect throw.
More of a straight-armed, long-range lob than an actual
throw, it was a slower, more looping and over-the-top kind
of action that let the weight of the clubhead lead the throw,
with the shaft trailing behind, not dissimilar to the way a
hammer throw in athletics leaves the chain in its wake. I
tried it a few times, and while it undoubtedly sent the club
higher and further it was only satisfying in the way neat
handwriting is satisfying. I can see that it plays a necessary
role in the club-thrower's armoury, but I would urge the

prospective thrower to consider its use carefully. We would-n't want to give the sport a good name.

It is with great pride, and tremendous shame, that I now confess to having invented a third club-throw, which appears here for the first time in public. (Please be advised this should only be attempted by advanced club-throwers with an unquenchably reckless desire to punish themselves for being so crap.)

The Snapper

Picture the scene: you've smothered your second into the face of a fairway bunker on a par-five when you only had a 5-iron in your hand and you were thinking birdie or even better which you seriously need because you've gone out in 46 which is all of your handicap right there and what's worse your inner thighs are beginning to chafe because you put on the jockeys that ride up by mistake …

Sometimes, throwing a club just doesn't seem enough. What you need is punishment. How does a £50 fine sound? Just the job? Excellent, that'll teach you.

All you have to do is throw the errant 5-iron down in front of you like it was a closed umbrella whose end you were trying to spear into the ground. If you get it just right you'll find that the clubhead thuds into the grass and the shaft snaps neatly in two. Now simply gather up the two halves, secrete them inside your bag, taking care to avoid any sharp edges, and present them to your friendly neigh-bourhood pro. You can either confess to breaking it yourself, or claim that you caught it on a root while playing a shot or, as I preferred, announce that you'd been struck by lightning.

While we're on the subject there is one other aspect of club-throwing that should be touched upon. Whether it serves as a warning, or merely as encouragement, is up to the reader.

For the ultimate in punishment to both yourself and your misbehaving club you could always throw the wretched thing somewhere you'll never get it back from. To hell with £50 fines, go the whole hog. Show it who's boss. Remove it from your life. Banish the bastard in perpetuity.

I discovered this extra level of abuse the day I inadvertently threw my 3-iron into an enormous rhododendron bush by the seventh tee on the Old. (That old pull-hook thing – gets me every time.) I delved and delved but was unable to find it before I had to catch up my long-suffering playing partners. For the next three weeks I snatched sixty seconds further rummaging every time I played the hole. I did find it in the end, but by that time it had gone a bit rusty. Still, serves the little bugger right.

From this it was but a small step to the deliberate tree toss. I can't remember the make of the putter but, in one of the few times I've used 'The Hammer', it was despatched with precision into the upper branches of a fir tree next to the fourteenth green. This would have been in the early 1980s and, for all I know, it's up there still.

The only other time that I deliberately purged myself of a club was notable for the multiple ways it suffered. I was always fascinated by the story of Rasputin's death and how the Russian authorities poisoned him; shot him; shot him again; then threw him in a river where, still not perished, he finally drowned. Well, I had a driver like that. After one appalling tee shot too many I decided enough was enough. For once, 'The Snapper' failed me (it doesn't work so well with woods), so instead I executed a perfect baseball swing at a tree trunk, catching the club just at the base of the shaft. To my annoyance it still didn't snap but, literally, wrapped itself around the tree, leaving the club with a comedy bend one end. Annoyed now, and wanting the club to just hurry up and die, I marched up the fairway (the fifteenth on the New) and threw it in the pond. Stone me if it didn't land on some reeds or something and remain three-quarters visible, poking up out of the water like some surreal golfing Excalibur.

I spent the next few minutes trying to snag it with a branch. I learnt later that this made the boys think that I had had a change of heart and was now making a sheepish attempt at retrieving the club, and indeed, the situation. Not quite. Once I'd snaffled the bastard I threw it straight back into the very middle of the pond where there was nothing to stop it sinking, and smiled through thin lips as it slipped beneath the murky waters to mock me no more.

The club-throw is rarely seen in today's professional game, and quite right too; it is a terrible example to set impressionable junior golfers and a disgrace to the spirit of the noble game. It's also, however, bloody funny to watch pro golfers losing it big time. As reprehensible as it is, the club-throw is a display of emotion, and as such, rarer on Tour than Levi 501s.

So visors off then to the following batch of hotheads who, in their own ways, flew the flag for short-tempered incompetents everywhere.

Tommy 'Thunder' Bolt

The Daddy of all club-throwers.

As one writer put it, 'Other golfers threw clubs, Tommy threw bags.'

Now, you may well have heard of Mr Bolt but what, like me, you may not have known is just what a great golfer he was.

Generally regarded as one of the purest strikers of a golf ball ever, he didn't tee it up on Tour till he was thirty-four, but then won twenty-five times in sixteen years. His finest moment was winning the 1958 US Open by four shots from Gary Player but a few years later, in the USPGA, and at the ripe old age of fifty-three, showed that he was still a class act by tying for the lead after sixty-three holes with a certain Jack Nicklaus in his prime. Bolt played the last nine in level par, but Nicklaus did it in 3 under and that was that.

And this is what I love about Tommy Bolt. He didn't have a shocking temper because he was rubbish, but because he was so good that imperfect shots offended him. Even Ben Hogan thought he was the bee's knees. 'If we could've just screwed another head on his shoulders, Tommy Bolt could've been the greatest who ever played,' Hogan once said.

The stories about him are legend. Like how he once had a 200 yard approach shot and asked his caddie what the club was.

'A 7-iron, Mr Bolt,' the boy answered.

'A 7-iron!' screamed Tommy. 'What makes you think I can get there with a 7-iron?'

CLUB-THROWING

A STEP-BY-STEP GUIDE

Illustrator: Ayşe Altinok.
Author appears as model.

THE WHIRLER

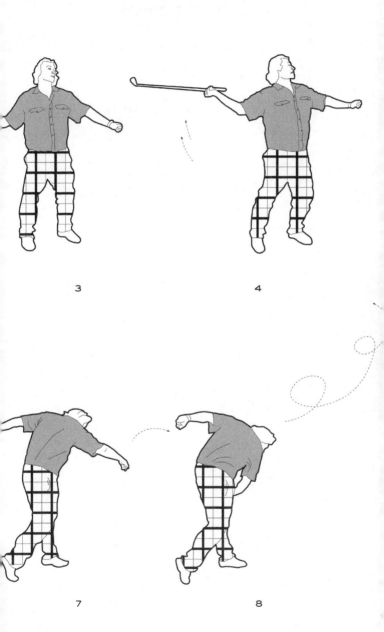

3

4

7

8

THE HAMMER

3   4

7   8

THE SNAPPER

1

2

5

6

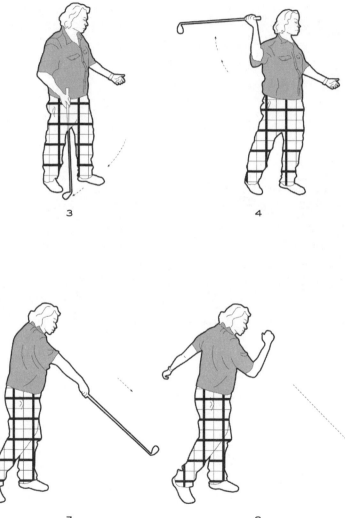

3

4

7

8

'Always throw clubs ahead of you; that way you don't waste energy going back to pick them up' – Tommy Bolt

'Because that's the only club you have left in the bag,' the caddie said.

Bolt claims that never really happened but some things are documented matters of record. Like hitting two drives into the lake on the eighteenth at the 1960 US Open, then throwing his driver in after them.

Like breaking a four-wood against a pipe.

Like stomping on the head of his driver with such venom that it stuck on his spikes and a spectator had to prise it off.

Like quitting in the middle of the 1962 Philadelphia Classic because no spectators clapped when he hit a beautiful shot over water that landed ten feet from the pin.

Like missing a short putt worth several thousand dollars, then, after chewing the grip of his club for a while, looking up at the heavens and thundering, 'Me again, huh? Why don't you come down here and play me? Come on, come on! You and your kid, too! I'll give you two a side and play your low ball!'

Like hurling his favourite driver into a canal, then hiring a diver to retrieve it for him, but spending $75 without success.

As he put it, 'I never threw a club that didn't deserve it.'

'The driver goes the shortest distance when you throw it,' he once said. 'The putter flies farthest, followed by the sand wedge.'

And his classic quote: 'Always throw clubs ahead of you; that way you don't waste energy going back to pick them up.'

Tommy Bolt thought that golf was a conspiracy and

that both the game, and the world, were against him. But he was wrong. As *Los Angeles Times* columnist Jim Murray wrote, 'The world loved Tommy Bolt. He was every man who ever missed a 2-foot putt, who wouldn't take a double bogey lying down. Like hackers everywhere, Tommy knew what a two-timing tart golf can be. He let the world know what a trollop she was.'

In 1957 the PGA adopted the 'Tommy Bolt Rule' prohibiting the throwing of a club. Quite correctly, they were worrying that Tommy's flying clubs were setting a bad example to the younger, more impressionable members of the tour. The day after the rule was passed, Bolt send his errant putter skyward once more. He wanted to be the first one fined under 'his' rule.

On another occasion he was fined $250, for 'conduct unbecoming a golfer'. Only this time it wasn't for breaking clubs, but breaking wind. Bolt lived up to his 'Thunder' nickname by letting one rip just as an opponent was putting and the gallery had fallen into a respectful hush. It upset the players, as well as some spectators, and Bolt was forced to cough up the fine.

Asked to comment on the incident, Bolt is said to have replied, 'The whole thing was blown out of proportion.'

Only Tommy Bolt has ever flown into a rage *before* he missed a putt. At the Masters once he landed his second to the first hole some thirty feet right of the flag. The more he studied the line, the more irritated he got at the outrageous rolls and contours of the green. Finally, he turned away, walked to the fringe of the green, and slammed his putter to the ground. A moment later, he missed the putt by a mile.

After he won the US Open and proved to the world, and himself, what a great golfer he was, he mellowed somewhat, and while he still threw the odd club here and there – usually there – Bolt claims that it was really only for the galleries.

'I just decided that golf wasn't worth breaking a blood vessel over,' he said. In fact, he started carrying a card in his pocket which he would show to everyone at the drop of a hat. It read: *'God grant me the serenity to accept the things I cannot change, the courage to change the things I can, and the wisdom to know the difference.'*

Aw. I love a happy ending.

Clayton Heafner

Clayton Heafner was not a happy camper, as evidenced by the trail of hurled and broken clubs he left strewn across the PGA Tour in the 1940s.

What separates Heafner from other club-throwers is that he didn't wait to hit a bad shot before getting angry; he was angry all the time. You could have offered him some cake and he would have exploded.

A radio announcer once asked the great American golfer Jimmy Demaret to name the player on the Tour who had the most even disposition. 'Clayton Heafner,' said Demaret.

'Heafner!' the announcer spluttered. 'Are you kidding?'

'No,' replied Demaret. 'He's mad *all* the time.'

His speciality was quitting, and it pains me to announce that I've just discovered he has comprehensively beaten my supposedly 'unbeatable' all-time walking-in record. Fair play to the guy, though, he once quit, on the first tee of the first round of the 1941 Oakland Open, without playing a single shot.

Apparently, when he arrived on the first tee he heard the announcer say, 'Ready to tee off is Clayton Heefner from Linville, North Carolina. Let's hope Heefner isn't going to have the same trouble with Oakland's trees that he had the year before.' The gallery laughed, remembering how Heafner had got his ball stuck in the fork of a branch the previous year, and had been forced to climb the tree to hit it.

When the announcer had finished his introduction, Heafner stormed over to him with veins bulging. 'My name's Heafner, not "Heefner". I come from Charlotte, North Carolina, not Linville. And as for staying out of your goddamn trees, I'm not allowing myself the chance to get into them.' He turned to his caddie and roared, 'Stick my stuff in my car.' Five minutes later, he was gone.

He even got mad when he was cheered on. Just as he was preparing to play a chip shot in the 1941 Masters, someone in the gallery called out, 'Get in there and pitch, Clayton, old boy. I've got five bucks on you.'

Heafner exploded. 'I'm shooting for $1,500 for myself and I should "get in and pitch" for you and your lousy five bucks? You're crazy.'

Lefty Stackhouse

He was an American touring pro during the late 1930s, early 1940s, and he blew his stack with every errant shot. The difference with Lefty was that he only vented his wrath at two things – his clubs and his body.

Lean and mean, Stackhouse would draw his own blood,

bruise his own body, and break his own bones if his golf dared to be less than perfect. In one tournament in Texas, Lefty walked off one of the greens and onto the next tee, placed his hand on the ballwasher and beat his fingers to a pulp with his putter, not stopping till he had broken several bones.

'One time when he missed a short putt, Lefty punched himself right in the jaw with an uppercut,' recalled former pro, and Masters winner, Ken Venturi. 'He hit himself so hard, he fell to his knees. Then he hit himself again and knocked himself out! Another time he missed a putt and took his putter and smashed it over his right hand. Now his right hand was all bloody, but Lefty wasn't finished. He took the putter in his bloody right hand and said to his left hand, "And you're not going to get away with it, either," and hit that hand.'

He had a special punishment all lined up for when he'd hit a bad hook. He'd glare at his too strong right hand as if it were disembodied, and smash it against the nearest tree, all the while shouting, 'Take that, you bastard of a hand! That'll teach you!'

After shooting an 80 in a tournament at Memorial Park in Houston, Lefty worked himself into such a lather that he jumped head first into a big bed of prickly rose bushes. His concerned playing partners tried to help him up as he lay spread-eagled, face down on a bed of sharp thorns. 'Lemme be, goddamn it,' Stackhouse moaned. 'Lemme stay right where I am.' So they did.

'Gentle' Ben Crenshaw

Why is he called 'Gentle' Ben, please? Does anyone know? Did he save an orphan from drowning when he was younger and now nobody has the heart to speak ill of him?

And didn't you just want to punch him on the nose during the Brookline Ryder Cup a few years back? There was something about him that week that was just insufferable: all that finger-wagging in press conferences, and stuff. But that's by the by. What we're really interested in here is the Muirfield Village Ryder Cup in 1987, and his infamous broken putter. True, technically not an actual club-throw, I grant you, but still a moment of hot-headed petulance with a golf club as the abused object of one's own inadequacies, so I think it qualifies, don't you?

The facts are that he walked off the sixth green having three-putted, whacked the putter in a fit of pique most unlike 'Gentle' Ben, only for the shaft to snap in two. *(Forgive the footballing analogy, but this whole 'Gentle Ben' thing is like when Peter Shilton was routinely beaten from thirty yards throughout the whole of the 1980s, only for ignorant commentators to continually splutter, 'Oh, good Lord, that's a fantastic strike from Brian Kilcline and, I have to say, you don't often see Shilton beaten from thirty yards.' The more it was said, the more credence it was given – despite all evidence to the contrary – and, of course, the more people who heard it and believed it, the more it was said, in a depressing spiral of something-or-other.)*

Now, I don't know about you, but I would pay top dollar to see the television footage of Crenshaw as his expression turned from one of disgust and anger; to alarm; then to horror; then alarm again; then disbelief; then anger at his caddie; then denial; then despair; then anger once more, then finally, grim-faced determination on a massive, heroic scale – which was pretty much how he stayed for the rest of the round, until his eventual demise to Eammon Darcy.

To be fair to the man, he did follow up his bad behaviour with quite the most dazzling display of putting dexterity under pressure that the game has probably ever seen. To putt with a 1-iron, on the final day of the Ryder Cup, and then hole loads of putts, including a crucial eight-footer on the eighteenth to keep the match alive, is almost beyond understanding. Had he won the match as well, the Americans would by now have introduced a Ben Crenshaw Day.

If a prize were awarded, however, for the best club-throw ever, it would be a hard man who didn't give it to my good friend, and *bon viveur*, Peter Lovatt. Playing at the Foxhills club in leafy Surrey, he dunched a chip shot and in a rare show of temper, launched into an interesting underarm version of 'The Hammer'. Employing two hands, and with no backswing at all, he simply lifted the offending club straight up into the air with all his might. It's a risky throw, this one, and not a technique I can officially sanction, for the club can easily fall back to earth and brain the unsuspecting thrower, still too consumed with rage to notice its descent. (Not unlike Jack Nicklaus' vertical hurl on holing the putt that won the 1970 Open at St. Andrews – the one that nearly added injury to insult for a cowering Doug Sanders.)

This time, though, the club came back down handle-first *and was helpful enough to spear itself directly into the correct divider section of his propped-up golf bag nearby*; going all the way down so that it ended up nestling in his bag as neatly as if he'd put it there by hand.

Superb. All the explosive release of a normal club-throw, with none of the sheepish going and fetching afterwards.

CHAPTER TWELVE: PUTTING IS AN UNFATHOMABLE BUGGER: PART FIVE

Let me just say, Nick Faldo is God. (It *was* Jim Leggett, remember, but he stopped playing.) His record; his approach to the game; his impressively chiselled hair; history has no option but to declare him one of the game's greats. He is also one of golf's great thinkers, and if there was one player who you think might have been granted an insight into the mysteries of putting, it's him.

Not so.

As the 1990s drew to a close, his once magnificent game was beginning to unravel. After another 70-something round, and another missed cut, he was talking to the press and complaining about his putting. In particular, he seemed to be going through a phase of all his putts coming up short. He then said what is possibly the stupidest thing ever uttered in a press conference.

'No matter what I do,' lamented Faldo, 'I can't seem to get the ball to the hole.'

There was a moment's silence, then one of the assembled throng, braver than the rest, piped up.

'Why don't you just hit it harder?'

By all accounts, Faldo was not impressed.

CHAPTER THIRTEEN: THE RISE AND FALL, AND FALL, AND FALL, OF A CHAMPION

D on't know about you, but of all the recent Open champions, I hold the biggest soft spot for the Australian Ian Baker-Finch, and his thrillingly laid-back triumph at Royal Birkdale in 1991.

It was a mixture of things, I think. Obviously, there was the head-shaking wonder of the golf he played on the weekend; the record 29 shots he took to skip through the front nine on the Saturday; the five birdies coolly bagged in the opening seven holes of the final round to sprint away from a field still doing their stretching exercises; the casual feat of finding every fairway and every green on the Sunday, like it was some kind of piddly pro-am or something; and, of course, the scarcely credible 64-66 weekend double-whammy. But there was other stuff too; the way he looked as happy and surprised as everyone else at what he was doing; the way that, during his glorious last day charge, he didn't feel the need to indulge in all that steely-eyed, sneery-mouthed, fire-breathing, fist-pumping, gee-up malarky that so many pros seem to use as a 'determination' pill; the way he just seemed like the nicest man to ever win the claret jug; and the way, in the television interview afterwards, his two-year-old daughter licked the microphone, thinking it was an ice-cream.

All the more shocking then to see him subsequently tumble down the world rankings like he'd stepped through a trapdoor. Not that I really knew the details; I was just aware that he wasn't playing as well as he could, and that this went on for some time, and then, just as I was thinking 'whatever happened to Ian Baker-Finch?' he suddenly popped up as a reporter at tournaments on American TV.

What I didn't know until recently, and I suspect you didn't either, was just how far he fell and how ghastly his tale is. And so I tell it here; not, I hope, to revel in a decent man's plight, but because it is ultimately a triumph of the human spirit; even if it doesn't have a traditional, storybook happy ending.

The day Ian Baker-Finch was proclaimed the champion golfer of the year he was handed two things: the silver claret jug … and a double-edged sword. If only he had seen his achievement the way others saw it – as a glorious coming together of his talents in a never-to-be-forgotten week – then what happened over the next six and a half years need never have happened at all. Instead, he saw it as a sign that he could be great. That if he could just click his game up one more gear then he could be a regular winner on Tour and a bookie's bet for every major. He knew he was a good golfer, but up until that July day he had never really felt himself to be deserving of a place on the top table, sharing salt and pepper with the likes of Norman and Faldo.

But now … now he had shown that he had what it took. Now he had won a ten-year exemption on the US and Australasian tours, and an annual invite to The Open that would remain until he was sixty-five years of age. Now he had the time and the opportunity, if he worked hard, to take his game to another level.

The working hard bit wasn't a problem. The Baker-Finches were a farming family who believed that nothing was given on a plate, and this work ethic had been instilled in Ian by a father who had filled his days as an electrician and sawmill operator, while simultaneously running a twenty-five-acre farm. Oh, and bringing up six kids. Anyway, Ian had already shown he was a grafter. He had a short game from 100 yards in that was the envy of his fellow pros, and he didn't get it through clean living and prayer. He forged it into his body through hundreds of lonely hours of relentless, remorseless practice, because he knew that was what it took.

And so, after the giddy euphoria of his Open triumph had faded, he took a cold, hard look at his game.

Temperament – check.

Short game – check.

A putter that works – check.

Length – it's a fair cop.

Baker-Finch had never been long. It's something you're either born with, or you're not, and common sense told him that no amount of green vegetables – or for that matter, practice balls – was going to change that. But yet … but yet … this little voice at the back of his head kept shouting over the top of common sense, telling him that without more length his stay at the top table would be for one meal only. And tomorrow they were having shepherd's pie with gravy.

So Baker-Finch started looking for extra length with a

swing that wasn't able to give it to him. He'd never had one of those almighty swipes that so many pros seem to have today. He had a smooth little backswing that served him just fine … until he went past it and discovered, hidden inside, its deformed twin brother – an ugly little snap-hook. It didn't happen that often, but it never sent a postcard in advance, and that kind of thing preys on a guy's mind. Now maybe, just maybe, he could have worked it out if he'd had the time, but Baker-Finch was the new Open champion. And a nice guy. Who couldn't say no. Awards dinners; interviews; autographs; speeches; business ventures – they all took him away from the day job; hitting golf balls. It used to take him half an hour just to get to the range; all his practice habits changed. Which, of course, happens to every Open champion to a greater or lesser degree; it's just that most of them aren't trying to fundamentally re-jig their swing at the same time. (They have, after all, just won the Open.)

The following year, the record books will tell you that Baker-Finch's season was no more than half-decent. Six out of ten. Must do better. He did win – in the 1992 Vines Classic in Australia – and he had a second on the US Tour, but fifty-eighth on the money list left him angry and disgusted. As the year turned he took two months off to practice every day and will himself to be better.

Baker-Finch had a target for 1993. It was an ambitious target and it very nearly came off. He wanted to finish in the top ten of every major. Sure enough, in each one, with one round to go, he was in with a chance. But each Sunday he stumbled, and plummeted down the leaderboard; his fragile, put-upon swing failing to stand up to the self-inflicted pressure. He won again in Australia – the Australian PGA – but not on the US Tour, where it really mattered.

Too proud to take 2-irons off the tee, he battled on.

As any golfer will tell you, too much theory fries your brain. Baker-Finch's was bubbling away nicely on a medium heat. He was hitting a lot of shots right, so he figured he'd make his swing flatter; which is all very well for the not very big Ian Woosnam, but Baker-Finch is tall, and tall golfers need a tall, upright swing. Undeterred, Baker-Finch proceeded to groove a swing flat enough to chop down a tree. As he himself admits, it was the biggest mistake he ever made. Soon, he was missing shots left *and* right, which is about as bad as it gets. He would stand on a tee and, short of picking it up and throwing it, he would have no clue how he was supposed to get that little white ball to finish on the fairway.

The tragedy was he had, by now, reached the point where he could no longer go back to his old swing. Golf swings live in our muscle memory. (It's why we can go months without playing, then hit a tee shot off the first that turns out to be the best swing of the day.) But Baker-Finch's body had simply tried out too many new variations for his muscles to have any hope of remembering the original. It was gone forever. If you think about it (and it's best not to really), this meant that he was no longer 'Ian Baker-Finch'. He was just another swing; just another player, living in the body of a major winner. No different from all the other wannabes. It was as though that magical week at Royal Birkdale had happened to someone else.

And this is possibly the saddest thing about his whole story. He will never again swing the swing that won an Open.

He did manage one last top ten finish – at the Masters of all places, in 1994 – but then placed only sixty-fourth the week after, and followed that with a depressing ten missed cuts on the bounce. He would play well in practice; play well in the pro-am; but then struggle to break 80 on the Thursday. Then he surprised everyone, including himself. He shot 67 in the first round of the World Series to find himself breathing down the leader's neck. False dawn. The next day he found a new way to fail: he took only twenty-one putts in eighteen holes, but lost all ten balls in his bag on the way to shooting 82 and coming second last. Something for everyone, there.

At the 1994 Hyundai Masters, he shot 66 in the pro-am, and set a new course record. The following day, he shot 81. At the 1995 Augusta Masters, he stayed on the range until he hit fifty perfect practice drives in a row. Then he walked to the first tee and pulled his opening drive so far left it landed on the ninth fairway.

And then there was that ten-year exemption. What most guys view as the ultimate golfing perk was, for Baker-Finch, just a cruel way of prolonging his agony in full view of the world. Other golfers now looked away when he swung, for fear that something might rub off. That hurt, but what ultimately hurt more was that so many also tried to help. Dozens of them would come up to him at tournaments and quietly proffer the swing thought that would give him back the life he loved. They only made things worse. When twenty different people give you twenty different tips (some of them the polar opposite of each other) how do you sort the life-saver from the waste-of-time?

Anyway, by now, Baker-Finch's problems were as much in his head as in his arms, legs and hips. In short, he was losing it. One of the basics of golf is to visualise the shot before you hit it. But Baker-Finch could not visualise a good shot; simply could not see it going where he wanted. He didn't see fairways, he saw trees and out-of-bounds. He couldn't see greens, only bunkers and Bermuda grass. You'd think that the law of averages would make *some* of his shots find their target – even if it was by accident – but the power of negative thinking beats everything.

1995 was not a good year. Baker-Finch played in twenty-four tournaments, and in twenty-four tournaments, he missed the cut. A quarter of all the rounds he played that year were in the 80s. He broke par only twice. He came in with an 85 at the Players Championship; shot 79-81 at the Masters (normally, the one event that didn't humiliate him); 84 at the Memorial; twin 81s at the Buick, and 84 at Disney. He averaged four penalty strokes per round.

In 1996 he played nineteen events. He made the cut just once. (History does not record how he felt on this red-letter day – joy, relief, or just sadness that he should be so glad to have achieved something so unremarkable.)

Meanwhile, Baker-Finch was trying everything he could. No coach was left unturned. Or caddy. Or sports psychologist.

Nothing helped.

He became the ultimate test of a guru's ability – could they solve the Baker-Finch puzzle? Could they be the one to crack it where the likes of Leadbetter and Butch Harmon had failed? Let's face it, they'd be set for life – the swing doctor with the miracle cure. Hardly surprising then that every time Baker-Finch trudged his way down to a practice range, he would soon find half-a-dozen strangers standing behind him with video cameras whirring. It seemed everyone wanted a permanent record of the worst swing of modern times.

The fates continued to find new ways to embarrass and humiliate him. A particularly good one was the Tour's habit of pairing major winner with major winner for the first two days. The last thing Baker-Finch needed was to hack it around with the likes of Jack Nicklaus and Arnold Palmer watching on, but that's what happened time after time. Playing with Nicklaus at the 1995 US Open at Shinnecock Hills, Baker-Finch scrabbled round in 83-82. (Afterwards, Nicklaus was moved to invite Baker-Finch to stay at his house for two weeks to try and sort him out. Baker-Finch turned down the offer.) Then came the single worst moment of the whole slump; played out in front of millions; in the major he had once made his own; at the home of golf; in the company of Arnold Palmer; on the widest, most easy- to-hit fairway in professional golf. On the first tee at St Andrews in the 1995 Open, Baker-Finch hit one of the hardest-to-believe shots ever seen by a champion – a pull-hook so severe that it crossed two fairways and went out-of-bounds on the far side of the eighteenth, 170 yards to his left.

(On top of everything, his visor fell off when he played the shot, tugged loose by a gust of wind just as he struck the ball. When have you ever seen that happen? As if hooking the hook to end all hooks wasn't bad enough, the golfing gods thought they'd make him look silly as well. I can still picture it – Baker-Finch holding his follow-through, torn between looking down for his visor, and keeping an eye on where his bad shot had gone, quite unable to credit that either had happened.)

Sadly, that pull-hook only kept the title of 'Worst Moment' for about six months. In that time Baker-Finch finally gave in and quit the US Tour before he became a gibbering loon. It was an agonising decision but he needed to go home; had to take stock. For six months solid he worked on his game away from the spotlight. The only competitive golf he played was with his pals for tuppence-ha'penny. He began to like the game once more – began to like himself once more – and little by little, he got better. And then it was Open time again. The week before the 1997 event he flew to Ireland to dip his toe into the water; a low-key pro-am in County Wicklow. He shot a very nice 69, thank you. Then he moved on to Royal Troon to do some TV work for ABC and prepare for the tournament proper, shooting right around par in his practice rounds and daring to think that maybe, possibly, surely, he had turned the corner. Or, at the very least, driven into good position on the dog-leg.

And then came the moment he had both craved, and dreaded. The velvet-voiced Ivor Robson, stalwart first tee starter for The Open since 1863, said the words that would either bring redemption, or relapse. *'On the tee, from*

Australia, and a former Open champion … Ian Baker-Finch.'
Cue applause. Cue practice swing. Cue …

A regulation par-four. Despite the occasion. Despite the crowds. Despite the pressure. No snap hook; no falling visor; no flushed embarrassment. Could this really be the round where Baker-Finch squares up to his demons, looks them full in the face … and pokes them in the eye?

No.

It was the round where his demons finally ripped out his heart and snapped it in two.

He double-bogeyed the second hole following a bad chip; doubled the sixth after a hooked drive; doubled the famous Postage Stamp par-three eighth after finding one of its devilish greenside bunkers; dropped three shots in a row to kick off the back nine; then double-bogeyed the thirteenth after another one of his patented hooks. The small amount of confidence he'd built up over the last six months ebbed right out of him and seeped into the unforgiving turf of Royal Troon. He actually thought about concocting a fictitious injury and pulling out mid-round but, although he knew people would understand, he couldn't bring himself to give up that way. Once a Baker-Finch, always a Baker-Finch.

And so he carried on. He triple-bogeyed the sixteenth by driving out-of-bounds right, then hitting his second equally far left. He double-bogeyed the par-three seventeenth. And, as he stood on the tee at the monster, 452-yard par-four eighteenth, a broken man, he did his maths.

Baker-Finch would need to hole his second shot for an eagle to keep his score under 90. He bogeyed it for a 92.

Still, he had at least introduced himself to a new experience. He had thought that he could never feel worse than after the infamous St Andrews shot, but no; walking up the eighteenth at The Open about to shoot 92 knocked it into a cocked hat. People rushed to line the fairway, straining to see the Open champion who could no longer play golf. Those 452 yards must have felt like ten miles. Eventually, in a daze, he pulled his ball from the hole, shook a few hands, signed his scorecard, and walked slowly into the clubhouse. A wreck, Baker-Finch made a beeline for The Champions Room (the room reserved only for past champions) as a sanctuary from everyone and everything. Once inside, he collapsed in a ball on the floor and simply cried his eyes out, cradled in the arms of his wife Jennie.

They stayed in there for forty-five minutes until Baker-Finch dragged himself to his feet, checked his face didn't look too splotchy, and did what no other professional sportsman would have done. He attended the press conference and answered whatever they wanted to ask him. 'I can't get any lower than this,' he told the room.

The WD that appeared next to Baker-Finch's name the next day was inevitable, even for someone as proud as he is. A man can only take so much. And so he went back to Australia and vowed to keep going, keep practising, work harder.

In November 1997, someone threw Baker-Finch a lifeline. Jack Graham of ABC Sports offered him a contract to be a full-time, on-course commentator. The only reason he didn't snatch his hand off there and then, taking a couple of fingers with it, was because … you've guessed it, he'd been working really hard on his game. He'd teamed up with a coach called Gary Edwin who had a different approach to all the others. He treated Baker-Finch like he was a beginner. Together they'd been practising sixty hours a week and Baker-Finch was beginning to trust the basic swing he'd been learning. Plus, there was a further complication. If he didn't play fifteen tournaments on the US Tour in 1998, he would lose his card; his exemption didn't come into it. The thing is, he'd given up on the Tour for the time being, so fifteen tournaments was pie in the sky. Which, if he harboured any notions of ever being a professional golfer again, left him with only one choice – to try and win his card back in the company of all the hungry, fearless young bucks.

His new coach had been testing his pupil out in the smallest, most insignificant pro-ams he could find (though even at these, word would get out and the rubber-neckers would descend to feast on their prey), and every now and then his pupil had done him proud. A 67 at one pro-am. An eight birdie round on his home course, Hope Island. That October, at a minuscule event somewhere or other, Baker-Finch had finished sixth and won £600. Not much really, but then it wasn't just money – it was Prize Money. Ian Baker-Finch was earning his living as a golfer once more.

He asked ABC for a bit of time to think about their offer and did what he was always going to have to do first. He entered a tournament on the Australasian Tour. He had to know whether the 'if-all-else-fails' swing he had been grooving was the real deal or not, and the Coolum Classic, just half an hour from his house, was the place to find out.

If he thought he'd be able to just sneak onto the course and play, he was wrong. The press had got wind and were out in full. On the morning of the tournament there were four articles about him in one paper alone. It was too much. After seven holes he was four over par. He double-bogeyed the eighth, hitting hooks all the way up it. When he put his first drive in the lake on the ninth, and then followed it in with his second, he quit before he hurled himself in as well. He walked in, announced that he had disqualified himself, and entered the press room with steam coming out of his ears. It was the day when he could bite his tongue no longer. When his pent up frustration either had to bubble over, or burst inside him.

'Why can't you leave me alone?' he demanded of the waiting reporters. 'Why does everyone have to have a photo of me? Why does everyone have to have quotes? Why does everyone have to know what I shot?' A press man tried to answer, saying that people were interested in him. 'Oh yeah,' said Baker-Finch. 'Like all the other sadists and people who want to see me do poorly.'

A week later, Baker-Finch quit professional golf, and made a phone call to ABC Sports. He wasn't saying he'd never play again, but he was sure as hell putting the clubs in the attic.

Since 1998, Baker-Finch has done more than twenty broadcasts a year for ABC Sports as an expert analyst and on-course reporter, and another six events for ESPN. He is heavily involved in course design and, by all accounts, his creation at The Golf Club Kennedy Bay, forty minutes south of Perth, is a must play, felt by many to be Australia's most links-like links. He was the Captain's Assistant to Gary Player at the 2003 President's Cup, is the charming host of numerous corporate outings and, when he can squeeze it in, manages the Greg Norman-designed Glades Golf Course on the Gold Coast.

Oh, and occasionally he plays competitive golf.

In 2001, Baker-Finch dusted his clubs off and played in The Mastercard Colonial, his first PGA event since 1997. He shot 74-77. It annoyed him that he missed the cut, but it didn't eat him up, and he slept well that Friday night. Each year he plays a tiny handful of events – sometimes scores well, sometimes doesn't – but at no point in any of them do his palms sweat, or does his mouth go dry, or does the fear creep back into his eyes. Giving up was the smartest move he ever made.

He may not have the silky swing he once had, but the old Baker-Finch is back again. Not the-out-in-29-at-the-Open Baker-Finch, but the laughing, smiling, happy-in-his-own-skin Baker-Finch. The one who loves golf. The handsome, decent family man who knows how lucky he is to make his living from the game. When he looks in the mirror these days, he likes what he sees – an Open champion who had some problems, gave it his best shot, and moved on.

Baker-Finch is in his mid-forties now, and the chances are that he will never again trouble the leaderboard in a golf tournament that means something. But is life really that cut and dried? Golf has already proved it can be a cruel game, maybe it can be a funny game as well.

Baker-Finch, if he wants to, can enter the Open for another twenty years. Who's to say that, one sunny July week sometime in the future, a certain lanky Australian won't get the sniff of adventure in his nostrils, find that his muscles can suddenly remember everything like it was yesterday, and make the unlikeliest, craziest, loveliest charge for victory this silly old stick and ball game has ever seen.

Well, since 1991, anyway.

CHAPTER FOURTEEN: **PUTTING IS AN UNFATHOMABLE BUGGER: PART SIX**

H ere's the thing:
When I try and putt correctly, with straight, V-shaped arms, firm wrists and a metronomic pendulum motion triggered by a simple rocking of the shoulders, I HAVE NO FEEL. Mechanics consume me, my arms feel as rigid as planks, and I am like a putting robot, only not in a good way. According to the textbooks I am doing the right thing, and if there were any youngsters watching, they would be well advised to tarry a while and study my stroke, but no matter how it looks, the fact is, me and the putt are not as one. We are as two, which, coincidentally, is how many putts I'm going to take. Unless it's three.

But when I adjust my stroke, get comfy and bring some feel in to it – hunched over a bit more, eyes right over the line, hands a bit looser, wrists a bit suppler, the mental sound of ball on cup ringing in my ears (*SFX: badok-adok-adok*) – I still can't consistently hole putts. This is because now MY TECHNIQUE STINKS.

I can't win.

It's catch 22.

Or putt 3.

CHAPTER FIFTEEN: PUTTING IS AN UNFATHOMABLE BUGGER: THE CHAPTER

I t was four feet long, the line was just right of centre, and for a moment there, it looked like just another putt.

I was playing in an annual twenty-a-side Ryder Cup-style match, last September, between English and Irish golfers – great fun, great craic, but important enough for it to matter who wins and who loses. My partner and I were one-up, and four tee shots of varying quality had just been struck to the short-ish, par-three fourteenth at Saunton Sands in North Devon, and as we strode up to the green I was wondering how the hell it was that we were ahead when neither of us was playing that great and one of our opponents was a seriously good golfer.

Their balls were side-by-side, twenty-five-feet from the hole and both of them faced a hellish double-breaker with one of those ridiculous Augusta-type slopes by the pin that required the ball to go past the cup, slow to a trickle, then actually come back towards the hole like there was a magnet in it being held by Bugs Bunny. It was the kind of putt that makes people offer you a pound if you hole it. (Or makes me offer people 5p, because I think that's quite funny.)

MY PARTNER, *STEVE HALL*, HAD HIT A BAD TEE-SHOT SOME WAY LEFT OF THE GREEN AND, ONLY BEING ABLE TO MAKE A PAR THREE AT

BEST, WAS, EFFECTIVELY, OUT OF THE HOLE AND NO USE TO MAN NOR BEAST. I emphasise this only because, in the aftermath of what happened next, this inescapable truth was conveniently forgotten when it came to the apportioning of blame.

As for my tee shot, well, after I had watched MY PARTNER, *STEVE HALL*, PULL HIS 7-IRON MOST GRIEVOUSLY, I hitched up my slacks, ignored THE UNBEARABLE PRESSURE HE HAD HEAPED UPON ME and knocked the ball to, yes, four feet. A terrific shot IN THE CIRCUMSTANCES, and followed straight after by our opponents' two blows.

So, AFTER MY PARTNER, *STEVE HALL*, HAD PLAYED A PITCH TO TWENTY FEET THAT COULD BEST BE DESCRIBED AS WORKMANLIKE, the real business began. The better player of our two opponents went first and hit his putt … more snakey than the really long snake that snakes from top to bottom in a game of Snakes and Ladders. Sure enough, it took the first break, took the second, slowed to a trickle, and reversed gently into the exact dead centre of the cup. The bugger was that it wasn't even a fluke, for the guy who stroked it was a five-handicapper who had been putting like a dream all round, and had obviously worked out the only way it was going to get into the hole.

What is it all the experts say about matchplay golf? Always assume your opponent is going to hole their putt; that way you won't be surprised when it happens, and you will be in a better frame of mind for holing yours. Apparently, the single worst response to an opponent's holed putt is,

'Cripes, that's torn it', so Bob Rotella wouldn't have been best pleased with my mental state as I prepared to tackle my four-footer – still for birdie, but now just for a half.

I'd been struggling with my putting for weeks and had been working my way through dozens of different strokes and postures and ball positions and elbow positions and backswings and follow-throughs and shaft angles and anything else you might care to mention. In this one round alone, I had experimented with two or three different methods, and as I stood over my innocuous little putt it all came home to roost.

For the first few seconds, it wasn't too bad. I took a couple of practice swings, all the while keeping in mind a positive memory of the previous day when, in an almost identical situation, I had holed the putt for the half and even put a decent stroke on it. But then I put my club behind the ball and entered a strange world of incompetence and incapability (Jane Austen's often overlooked last novel).

I have read that when people have the yips they find it almost impossible to take the putter away from the ball; that, no matter how they try, they simply cannot start the stroke. Well, this wasn't like that. I had no problem taking the club away from the ball, I just didn't know what to do with it when I did. It suddenly struck me that not only did I not know what would be the best stroke to employ, I wasn't even sure, should I find a stroke, that I could then go ahead and execute it. As soon as I moved my Mizuno blade, my arms would embark on whatever stroke they fancied, and I could only pray that it was conducive to the shot at hand. In effect, I simply didn't know *how* to make a backswing on this putt. And, alarmingly, the same thing applied to the stroke through the ball. I hadn't the foggiest what I should do. I could see the ball, I could see the hole, I just couldn't see how I should move my arms and hands to allow the putter to get one into the other.

Somewhere in my head I became aware that time was passing and that I would have to do something. So I made my move, unaware of what it would entail, or where it would lead.

I did, at least, hit the ball, and it wasn't a yip in the classical sense as my muscles didn't spasm and the putter didn't jerk and the ball didn't end up fifteen feet past the hole.

It finished two feet short.

On a four-foot putt.

Through nerves, fear and what snappy phrase-makers call 'paralysis by analysis', I had contrived to decelerate the club so much that I had only just reached the ball on the downswing, with barely enough strength to send it on its way. If I remember correctly, I stared for a second at the ball, then looked at my playing companions and said, 'I appear to have had a mechanical breakdown'. It was good of me to tell them this, but probably not necessary.

Sure enough, we went on to lose the match on the last hole, making my two-foot reverse yip on the fourteenth crucial to our eventual demise. Still, let's look on the plus side. I brightened everyone's day no end back at the clubhouse, courtesy of my partner's strangely gleeful retelling of the incident, and I am now forced to acknowl-edge an inescapable truth.

I cannot putt.

The bugger is, I don't acknowledge it. It's one thing to admit it here, but quite another to do anything about it, and deep down, I am quite happy to ignore all the available evidence and pretend that I don't have a problem. I know me, and I know that the next time I play, it will be with the genuine belief that the stroke will be smooth, the mind will be uncluttered, and the putts will drop. My trouble, in life as well as golf, is that I tend to assume things will just be okay. I don't just see the glass as half-full, I also think it's great that it's got water in it 'cos water's really good for you. So when it comes to putting, I spend an ultimately useless two minutes on the putting green, and then stroll onto the first tee blithely assuming that the ball will just find its way into the hole.

It doesn't help that other people also seem to think I'm a good putter. I was at a party the other day and a good friend mentioned to someone I was meeting for the first time that I had a really good short game. The weasel in me smiled and went along with it in an 'aw, shucks' kind of way. The golfer in me wanted to hold up a glass, tap it vigorously with cutlery, ask for everyone's attention, and then announce in a firm voice, 'MY NAME IS RICHARD RUSSELL, AND I AM A BAD PUTTER. IT'S BEEN FOUR MONTHS NOW SINCE I'VE DRAINED A PUTT OF ANY LENGTH OR SIGNIFICANCE.'

It wasn't always like this. There was a time when I ruled the greens; when putting was the best bit; when I practised like there was no tomorrow.

Let's go back to my childhood … *childhood … childhood … childhood …*

My first putter wasn't just any old putter; it was Clive Clark's old putter. You know, Clive Clark, the guy I mentioned earlier. Sunningdale Pro; Tour Pro; Walker Cup player; Ryder Cupper; eleventh in the 1972 Open; hole-in-one at the sixteenth in the 1968 Masters; holed bunker shot at the very first Cadet Clinic at Sunningdale in 1975; BBC on-course roving reporter in the 1980s.

Okay, he wasn't a superstar, but he was a pro who'd done some funky things and that was good enough for a thirteen-year-old me. And now I had his actual putter; the one he used as a pro. The putter he didn't even need to take out of his bag that day at the Masters. A gold Bullseye with that distinctive slopey shape; like a snail without its shell on.

I've still got it, in a cupboard next to some of my old clubs that I can't seem to throw out (hey look, a wooden wood!), but over the years it's taken a frightful battering. The brassy gold has now darkened to a colour that doesn't actually have a name, and it's covered in tiny chips, lines and lesions. It looks like the huge thumb of a wrinkly-skinned, worryingly tanned, elderly Floridian golfer. You couldn't putt with it now, either. You'd be scared its pock-marked surface would send the ball off at forty-five degrees, and there's something about that Bullseye shape that just doesn't feel right any more (and this in the era of putters shaped like branding irons). It's so low slung, it looks like it could pass clean under the ball. But for a while there, we made a great team, and if only it was remotely interesting to read about, I'd take you through some of the putts we've holed together.

I got it out the other day and stroked a few imaginary

putts on the carpet with it, for old time's sake. And you know what?

It felt horrible. It looked horrible. It seemed inconceivable that I could ever have holed anything with it.

How can this be?

What does it all mean?

Simple.

Putting is an unfathomable bugger.

And you can quote me on that.

(In fact, I'd rather like it if you did. I've always wondered how it is that quotes get into circulation, and it grieves me to see so many dull quotes given house-room. Do people send their quotes to a Central Quote Office for valuation and subsequent distribution? Or do you just have to keep repeating your phrase in the hope that, eventually, people start taking it up? Call me fanciful, but in five years time I'd like to click onto Google, type in 'golf quotes', and see *'Putting is an unfathomable bugger'*, right next to Mark Twain's *'Golf is a good walk spoiled.'* What do you say? Let's make it happen.)

Like most golfers, there was a time when I putted really, really well. It was called my youth, and funnily enough, it coincided exactly with the time when I was always up at the club and always on the putting green. How good was my putting? Well, God help me, at one point I can distinctly remember saying to Mark Trickett that the idea of me three-putting was absurd because, in order for me to commit such an atrocity, 'I would have to hit two bad putts … in a row'. I can still remember the genuinely incredulous tone I used when delivering that last '… in a row'.

I also remember strolling around the practice green one day and hitting upon a revolutionary way to beat my course record of 8-under par. (Every hole being a par-two.) I decided that unless I holed-in-one the first three holes, I would simply start again. Miss the first; start again. Hole the first, miss the second; start again. Hole the first, hole the second, miss the third; start again. (And these were putts of around twenty feet we're talking about. Honestly, the bloody gall.) Annoyingly, I holed the first three a number of times, but on each occasion, failed to improve upon my course record. I think it was God's way of telling me not to be an insufferable little twat.

The secret, I now realise, was that when I started playing golf I paid no attention to the mechanics of putting. I simply gave it no thought whatsoever. One day, Mark T asked me how I putted and I was surprised to find myself unable to answer. It had never occurred to me before. I thought about it for a while before replying, 'I dunno ... I just hit it'.

Don't get me wrong, it wasn't so much that I holed everything in sight at that time, but more that I seemed to have complete confidence in almost every putt. Anything between three feet and fifty feet was holeable, especially when I employed my dotted line mental homing device. This was a visualisation technique that was borrowed wholesale from CBS 'Action-Track'; a viewer's aid that the American networks used to use during the American majors. Should Gibby Gilbert, or Hubert Green, or Ed Sneed, hole a curling thirty-footer, CBS would re-play it, tracking the ball's path with a white dotted line so you could see exactly how the ball had curled into the hole.

Trouble is, it was shit. It didn't really show you anything you hadn't already seen with your own eyes, and it was even more useless if the putt was only a little bit bendy. (Where's the interest in seeing a relatively straight line continue to extend in a relatively straight line towards a hole that we already know the ball will fall in to?) No, the only thing it was good for was helping you to hole your own curly-wurly twenty-footer. Just send a mental dotted line from your ball to the hole along the line of borrow, and hey presto, it's like you've laid a groove in the green which the ball has no option but to follow till it topples into the cup. It really was a great way to visualise the putt and I have no clue why I don't use it any more.

Tiddlers were different. Tiddlers were the one putt where my wristy action and looky-uppy head movement put the outcome in serious jeopardy. I wasn't entirely hopeless, but I missed enough of them to open the door to Mr Doubt – sometimes even inviting him in to stay for supper. And, of course, once you're pals with Mr Doubt, he pops round all the time, whether you want to play or not. Next thing you know, he's brought round his trouble-making colleagues, Mr Sullen, Mr Swear, and Mr Club-Throw.

Luckily, I had a plan. It wasn't cunning – it was stupid – but, amazingly, it worked.

I called it 'The Philosophical-er'. (Something to do with the golfer needing to feel philosophical about the putt, and its eventual outcome, rather than worrying about it, which only increases his chances of missing it. Look, I told you it was stupid.)

What I did was, whenever I had an important tiddler to hole, I took a couple of practice putts while simultaneously announcing to all and sundry, 'Right, this looks like a philosophical-er'. I then immediately hit the putt – almost on the '-er' of 'philosophical-er'. This served to fool my body into not realising I was putting at all. The key, I realised, was in the physical act of speaking out loud. You cannot say, in a loud voice, 'Right, this looks like a philosophical-er' while, at the same time, filling your head with the usual crap that a short, eminently missable putt normally throws up. e.g. the mechanics of the stroke; the ghastly implications of missing; the probability of your limbs not doing what they're told; the wisdom of Gary Player's tip about never hitting a putt of less than six feet outside the hole; the nagging doubt that you should have positioned the number on the ball so that it was facing towards the hole and not away, because you've missed your last three holeable putts and they all had their number facing away, and maybe that's the reason you're missing them; etc., etc., etc.

I can honestly say that I cannot remember ever missing a putt when I employed this somewhat idiosyncratic technique. It was like I was beating the system. And, as they say on the cover of blockbuster diet books, it can work for you too. Beware though; it is quite difficult to execute if you're playing with strangers, or there's a crowd of some kind. You have to weigh up the merits of holing the putt, against the quizzical looks your exclamation will generate.

Still not sure? Look at it this way: what's the worst that can happen? You miss the putt. But, then, that's what you're already doing, so what have you got to lose?

If it helps, you don't have to say, 'Right, this looks like a philosophical-er.' You could just say whatever you want.

'Is it me, or have Y-Fronts had their day?'

'Apparently, George Washington had wooden teeth.'

'Crikey, I'm never going to hole this.'

(I like that last one. It's like it's taking the whole psychological, putt-beating, mind game thing to its ultimate ironic conclusion. Every time you face a tiddler, announce that you're going to miss it, but then never do. Talk about laughing in the face of fear. How much would that piss off the God of Missed Putts? Or Forfuchsachus, to give him his full Greek mythological name.)

So, to sum up: once I was good at putting, now I'm not. And George Washington shouldn't have eaten so many sweets.

So what's the moral? Where's the lesson? Where do we (I) go from here?

Well, at the risk of repeating myself, it's simple.

Putting is an unfathomable bugger. Just accept it and move on. In fact, don't just accept it, embrace it. Putting will always be an uncrackable puzzle to all but the chosen few, so why not just become fascinated by it, instead of worrying about something that's beyond your control? Doesn't it follow that you'd end up putting better? It's all very well having a good stroke, but that means nothing if your head's not right.

If you want my advice (which, I would suggest, you really, really don't), you should approach every putt with the faintly detached air of a man conducting an experiment on The Open University. Think of this approach as 'The Philosophical-er' taken to its ultimate conclusion.

'Ah, now here we face another one of those awkward thirty-foot lag putts. Interesting. We know from bitter experience that pace is everything on these putts, yet having the feel for them is very difficult. Let's send the ball on its way and see what happens. (SFX: the sound of balata on Scotty Cameron insert.) *There she goes … she's rolling nicely … and … she's gone in the hole. Interesting.'*

When pros say that they were 'really in the zone today' how do we know that this isn't the zone they mean? The Open University Zone. There's no doubt they do something to detach themselves from the pressure.

There's brilliant black and white footage of Arnold Palmer winning the Masters by holing a short, but missable, putt that he knows is for the title. The interesting thing is his reaction when the ball drops. Without changing his expression, he just steps forward, nonchalantly picks the ball out of the hole, and takes a couple of steps away. Suddenly, his legs buckle and he staggers a bit before beaming broadly and furiously pumping the outstretched hand of his playing partner. It's obvious – he was in The Open University Zone.

'Hmm … I seem to have left myself a four-footer to win the tournament. Interesting. It may be short but they have been missed before, though not usually for such a massive prize. I wonder whether, amid all the pressure, I can still execute a solid stroke. (SFX: the sound of Dunlop 65 on blade putter.) *Interesting. The stroke was good and the ball has indeed gone in the hole. That's very satisfying and completely justifies my decision not to use that putter in the garage shaped like a …* HOLY SHIT, I'VE WON THE MASTERS!'*

You may scoff, but if it's good enough for Arnie …

CHAPTER SIXTEEN: CHICKEN AND CHIPS, OMELETTE AND CHIPS

Near the end of Indian restaurant menus they perform a curious (but rather admirable) service where they add some dishes to the menu that are only there for people who don't fancy the Indian food. In my experience, it's usually chicken and chips, and omelette and chips.

Quite why you'd be going into an Indian restaurant to eat if you didn't like Indian food is another matter. Perhaps you're courting a young lady who particularly likes Indian cuisine, and you don't want to disappoint. Or maybe you sat down with every intention of ordering the Lamb Rogan Josh, when your attention was caught by the chicken and chips option and now, through the power of auto-suggestion, you find you can't resist.

It's certainly a puzzle, yet it's also an extremely considerate thing for them to do, and it makes me want to do the same. You never know, there may well be people reading this book who don't much care for golf. Perhaps they're in prison and have read everything else in the library – even the Maeve Binchys. Perhaps they've mistakenly purchased the book on the assumption that it was something to do with David Yip, the one-time actor who played that Chinese detective fella on the BBC a while back.

Whatever, I'd like now to offer up two helpings of alternative fare.

Dame Edna Everage was once asked what made her laugh.

'Other people's misfortune, mostly,' she replied immediately.

And she's right, dammit; which means that, as much as this chapter seems like the perfect opportunity to drag you through some of my many genuine moments of sporting flair unconnected with golf, I'm not going too. As much as I'd like to prove that under this flabby exterior there beats the heart of a gifted sportsman, I must resist. As much as I really, really want to show off ... I shan't. So that's no re-telling of the twenty-five-yard, swivelling, overhead bicycle-kick goal for the Under-11's that compelled the sports master to clean my boots for a week, in a strange 'I'm-not-worthy' gesture. No shot-by-shot re-enactment of the last-gasp, do-or-die, eight ball pool clearance in the final frame to win my work team the whole damn match by a single point. No gleeful description of the flick-up, turn and half-volley at hockey that screamed into the far corner (a carbon copy of Justin Fashanu's sublime left-footed screamer for Norwich in the 1980s, footie fans). Not even a brief and business-like recounting of the fast ball that clean-bowled a village cricketer and, in the process, sent one of the bails spinning backwards with such force that when it struck our wicket-keeper on the head, it actually concussed him.

No, I shall mention none of those things. Instead, I shall dredge up two particularly painful memories, purely for your entertainment; memories that, until today, I had buried deep, deep, deep in my subconscious. Times when I tasted, not glory, but agonising defeat.

Interestingly, of the two times, only one of them tasted like chicken.

Chicken and Chips

It was 1970; I was eight years old, and in my first year at Stubbington House Preparatory School (only famous old boys, Scott of the Antarctic and Lance Percival, the toothy, upper-class twit comedy actor of the 1960s and 1970s – unsurprisingly, it was only Scott of the Antarctic who got the portrait and plaque, though Lance Percival did once land on the front lawn in a helicopter which, frankly, made him more of a hero to us boys than some guy who found a pole in the snow). Along with everyone else in my year, I was standing around in shorts and vest waiting for something called the Junior Cross-Country Race to begin. I'd never done a cross-country race before, so I figured I'd just tag along at the back, and see how it went.

Suddenly we're off; a tide of wee, skinny boys hurling themselves down the main drive. All went well to start with, but after a while I began to get a bit frustrated as everyone seemed to be going really slowly. I decide to overtake a few. And so it was that, unwittingly, I began to make my way through the field. I kept expecting to get tired, but it never happened and, after a bit, I came across a bunch of boys who didn't have anyone in front of them at all. It suddenly struck me that these must be the leaders ... I was running with the leaders!

Trouble was, this lot weren't running fast enough either; so I pulled out and started overtaking them as well. The next few seconds form one of the most cherished moments of my life. I passed these boys as if I had a rocket on my back and they were running in treacle, yet I wasn't even remotely puffed. It was effortless. I was flying. Thirty-two years later I can remember exactly the astonished joy I felt as I discovered I could run like the wind, and how satisfying it was to be so as one with my body. It was the only time I have ever felt such physical perfection and, even as I write, the memory of it is causing me to choke up a bit.

The reason this glorious feeling only lasted a few seconds is because, as I drew level with the leading runner, a boy called Black, I suddenly realised I didn't have the faintest idea where we were going. I had no clue what the course for this race was. Well, why would I? I'd had no intention of trying to win it. When I woke up that morning I didn't even know I could run this fast, so why would I have paid attention when the sports master took us through the route? Reluctantly, I folded in the wings on my feet, eased down and snuck in behind Black, planning to stick with him all the way until I caught sight of the finish line, then pull out and sprint to victory.

At this point we were at the topmost part of the school grounds, by the cricket nets. We then turned back towards the school building and ran across what, in the summer, is the First XI cricket pitch. We reached a path at the back of the school and, without warning, Black suddenly veered off to the right down towards a small courtyard. Instinctively, I stayed on his shoulder.

I was still on his shoulder as he ran up to a door, opened it, ran into the actual school building and down a corridor.

Where we bumped into a teacher who looked at us like we were a side salad he hadn't ordered, then started shouting.

'What the hell are you boys doing inside the school? Get back outside at once you dozy fools, and re-join the race!'

We turned and fled and ran back outside, but it was too late. There was a steady stream of boys running past us and down the gravel road that ran along the side of the school. The road we should have taken all along. As I sprinted past my schoolmates in a futile attempt to catch up with the leaders, I couldn't help but have a couple of questions nag away at me.

WHAT THE FUCK WAS BLACK PLAYING AT? WHAT WAS GOING ON INSIDE HIS STUPID, THICK SKULL? WHERE EXACTLY DID HE GET THE IDEA THAT A CROSS-COUNTRY RUN PROBABLY INCLUDED THE OPENING OF A DOOR?

I had to admit, there was also one more question that needed asking.

WHY THE HELL DID YOU FOLLOW HIM, YOU STUPID ARSEHEAD?

To which I can only reply that it all happened so fast your honour, and that the courtyard seemed like it could just about be part of a cross-country run, and by the time the idiot had opened the door it was just my momentum keeping me going, and anyway, by that stage, the damage was done.

I must have overtaken a dozen runners before finally crossing the finish line well behind the winner, about as upset as a little boy can be. To experience the wonder of running so effortlessly fast, and have it all come to nothing in such an absurd way, was too much for the eight-year-old me to take.

And Black, if we ever meet again, you're gonna get a Chinese burn you'll never forget.

Omelette and Chips

I was fielding at first slip for a local pub cricket side, three years after I'd left school.

(A word of advice: nobody likes an all-rounder in a pub cricket team. You can either bat or bowl, but not both. We're very happy to let you bowl first change, Richard, but if we let you bat at your normal no. 5 what happens to Barry? He can't bowl for toffee, and despite the fact that he can't really bat either, we have to put him up the order or he doesn't feel involved and that won't do; after all, the guy's been turning out for us for years. Same goes for Ted, Pete, and Lumpy, I'm afraid. Will No. 10 do?)

Up at the wicket, there was an interesting batsman/bowler duel going on. One of their openers was a guy in his fifties; a solid, experienced bat, but obviously intimidated by our young seventeen-year-old quickie. And with good reason; this kid was fast. Which in turn meant that we slips were way back from the wicket.

Anyway, they sussed each other out for a couple of overs and then, out of the blue, our quickie sent down a well-disguised slower ball. This completely threw the batsman who stepped back to just block it down onto the ground, but got his timing all wrong (which is, after all, the whole point of a quickie bowling a slower ball) and only succeeded in dolly-ing it right up in the air, straight in front of him. He was safe though, because nobody was near enough to catch it.

Next ball the bowler is running in when I get the strange feeling that he is going to bowl exactly the same ball again. I don't know why I thought this. No coaching manual would recommend bowling two successive slower balls – you have lost the element of surprise after the first one, the batsman would be ready for it. But something told me that the lad was going to do it again. For one, he was young and raw, and somehow I couldn't ever see him tucked up in bed reading a coaching manual. Also, he was quite cocky, and after making the batsman get all panicky and flustered the previous ball, I sensed that he wanted to fool the old boy again; and as soon as possible.

So I did something no slip should ever do. In the bowler's last few strides I started moving in towards the batsman. I had to. He was a serious, experienced cricketer (I could totally see *him* curled up in bed reading a coaching manual), and if I was right, he would never be expecting two slower balls in a row. And if it *was* a slower ball, then there was also a chance that the batsman might react as badly a second time, and repeat his knocked-up, forward defensive, scaredy-cat prod – which, in turn, meant that I needed to be nearer to him to stand any chance of catching it. (Phew. Funny how what only takes a split-second to occur in real life, takes so bloody long to explain in words.)

And so it came to pass, exactly as I had foreseen. The bowler bowled another slower one, the batsman panicked in exactly the same way as before, prodding the ball meekly up in the air, and Nostradamus here, already moving towards the wicket in anticipation of my hunch paying off, broke into a mad dash to get to the slowly arcing ball. Now, I've always quite liked throwing myself around while playing sport, which was lucky because this called for a ninety-degree, full-length job. With the rapidly approaching ground the bookie's favourite to win the race to the ball, I hurled myself …

… and caught the bugger, one-handed, at full-stretch, an inch from the ground.

Only for it to jiggle out of my hand a millisecond later, as I crashed to the ground. There was no way I could hurl my hefty frame through the air without some kind of seismic activity occurring on landing – activity that simply made it impossible to stop the ball getting knocked out of my still-trying-to-grasp-it-properly hand.

It was death or glory, and the sporting gods had spoken. Death.

I had very nearly caught a slip catch, off a fast bowler, *three feet in front of the batsman.* I had very nearly pulled off one of the most intuitive, most daring, most impossible catches you could ever wish to see.

Very nearly. I think they're the key words here, don't you?

So what was the point of that then, God? What was the point of granting me the vision to see that such a catch was even possible, but then not making me good enough to catch the bloody thing?

Sometimes, you really make me mad, you little tinker.

CHAPTER SEVENTEEN: **MOE NORMAN IS THE MAN**

I n the end, it's always Nicklaus' eighteen majors that settles it. Ask anyone to name the greatest golfer ever, and the same half-dozen names will invariably get bandied around (Jones; Nicklaus; Palmer; Hogan; Hagen; Woods; Player at a pinch), with the winner inevitably coming down to a shoot-out between Messrs Nicklaus and Woods. And while it may not be this way forever, it's always those eighteen majors that do for Woods in the end.

But what if we settle this argument a different way? What if the greatest golfer ever was, literally, the player who played the greatest golf, and not just the one who happened to triumph most often in a handful of pre-selected tournaments?

If you forget putting, which is a game within a game, the hardest part of golf is keeping the ball straight; controlling the ball; getting it to do what you want, and go where you wish. And if you agree with that, then there can only be one contender. The facts speak for themselves.

The greatest golfer who ever lived is a Canadian called Moe Norman. And the fact that you have, in all likelihood, never heard of Moe Norman is one of the game's great injustices, and one that this chapter, in its own little way, hopes to address.

So who is Moe Norman? How good was he? What did he do? What did he win? What's all the fuss about?

Well, as tempting as it is to just launch into story after story of Moe's legendary shot-making skills, there's one thing you need to know first, and the best place to start is Moe's favourite place on earth: the practice ground.

Moe Norman is seventy-five years old and hits the ball as well today as in his heyday on the Canadian Tour. He can do this because he has the Holy Grail – the most repeatable golf swing the game has ever seen. A swing that means he can hit it dead straight, every single time. (Or fade it, or draw it, whatever he fancies.) And this, in turn, is because he invented it himself. And by invented, I don't just mean he put the odd kink or loop in it. No, he took the golf swing apart and started again, based on his own theories of how the ball should be hit. And all this as a teenager, too. While other kids were goofing around and looking to get laid, the seventeen-year-old Moe Norman had already found his vocation in life: how to hit a golf ball straight. Every day he hit 800 balls on the driving range, studying every one of them, and tinkering with his swing accordingly. The better he got, the more he went his own way, and slowly but surely he perfected his unique move.

We could take ten pages to dissect Moe's incredible and individual swing but essentially it boiled down to a few fundamental things.

A really wide stance with ramrod straight legs. It lost Moe distance but he didn't care because it made him feel planted and he couldn't twist, so the clubhead could always come back on line.

Arms that were rigid and stretched right out. This meant the ball had to be further away, but also meant that his left arm formed an exact straight line with the club, making him the only golfer to swing on a single axis. (The rest of us make that divining rod 'Y' shape with our arms and club.)

The club in the palm of the right hand, not the fingers. This ensured that it couldn't twist and that the clubhead stayed square, always pointing at the flag.

The club placed twelve inches behind the ball at address. A genius idea that guaranteed every backswing started low and slow.

The grip held like a vice with the left hand. Forget that holding it like a bird nonsense – this prevented the club from wavering on the backswing, giving a wide and repeating swing arc.

Three-quarter backswing. Short and controllable, it doesn't let the club even think about moving off line.

Grip down the shaft with every club. If it makes a chip easier to control, why wouldn't it make all the other shots more controllable too?

Swing straight back and straight through. Moe used to place coins behind and in front of the ball and get the club to pass over both of them. The straighter the swing, the straighter the shot.

If Moe had one single thing he believed in, it was that you had to keep the clubface on line with the target, both before and after impact, for as long as possible, as the swing quirks above all testify to. Basically, golf was all about hitting the ball at a target, so why not swing the club in a way that achieved this?

The important thing to realise here is that Moe Norman is not like other golfers. (Nor indeed, other men, but we'll get to that.) He wasn't just someone who got good by practising a lot, like Hogan, but rather someone who dared to question the immutable laws and theories of golf, and was then smart enough to do it better himself. He saw the golf swing as having a job to do and being elegant wasn't it. Yes, his swing was ugly, but he didn't care, not when he could land it on a buttercup from 200 yards. And then knock it off the buttercup with his next ball.

The fact is, everything stems from Moe Norman's homemade swing. If he'd swung a club like you and me, then we wouldn't be talking about him now. And I wouldn't be able to list here, in one great big glorious gush, the stuff he's achieved and the incredible things he's done.

- He's had fifty-four tournament victories.
- He's had seventeen hole-in-ones. (Eight of them going straight in on the fly.)
- He's had four albatrosses.
- He's set thirty-three course records.
- Four of these are at 61.
- Three are at 59.
- That's right, 59.
- Early one morning Moe was playing a singles round at Tomoka Oaks in Daytona Beach, Florida with a buddy of his. On the tenth hole he hit three drives. As they walked up the fairway his partner thought he saw a big mushroom in the middle of the fairway. As they got closer he saw that it wasn't a mushroom, but three golf

balls … touching. They were Moe's three drives, and they had been hit so identically straight that each ball had ended up touching the other two. You could actually see the lines in the dew where they had rolled up against each other.

• When Moe got to the eighteenth tee of the 1971 Quebec Open he was leading the tournament by a stroke. The eighteenth was a tough hole, 440 yards with a green guarded by a lake. Norman smashed a drive then drilled a 3-wood fearlessly onto the green, but for some reason, the gallery didn't clap. Moe asked a marshall whether anyone else had hit the green in two that day and the marshall confirmed that they hadn't. This annoyed and perplexed Moe who kept saying out loud 'Why didn't they clap?' and then proceeded to hit his putt without lining it up or even breaking stride. It missed by a mile. 'Why didn't they clap?' he asked again, as he casually missed his next putt as well. Now he had a three-footer to tie but the crowd's reluctance to applaud seemed to be the only thing on his mind. To the gasps of everyone watching, he missed the short one too and threw away the tournament. As he left the green he could still be heard muttering about the crowd. Fast forward to the following day. With the same partner, Moe was playing a practice round for the Canadian Open at the Richlieu Valley Golf Club. The tenth tee was near the clubhouse and as he walked to it a bunch of reporters clustered round him, asking sarcastic questions about his putter and whether he was planning any four-putts that day. As they laughed, Moe just strode past them and onto the tenth hole, a huge 233-yard par-three. He grabbed his driver and blasted a shot away. He watched it for two seconds then, while it was in the air, turned round, folded his arms and announced, 'I'm not putting today.' The ball landed softly on the green, rolled only a few inches … and, as predicted, fell into the cup for a hole-in-one.

- In the 1954 America's Cup Moe was one down after thirty-four holes of his thirty-six hole match against the No. 1 US amateur Bill Campbell. It was the biggest match of Moe's career thus far. Campbell played first to the par-three sixteenth and hit it two feet from the stick. He then made some sarky comment about how it was now going to be a tough hole for Norman to win. So Moe stepped onto the tee, knowing he would have to actually play for a hole-in-one. A few seconds later, his tee-shot landed four feet past the cup and sucked back into the hole for the win he was going for. He went on to win the match. (Question: can a hole-in-one be a fluke if you're aiming for it? Discuss.)

- Competing in a tournament in Toronto, he came to the eighteenth hole needing a birdie three to set a new course record. 'What is this hole?' he asked his caddie. 'A driver and a 9-iron,' the caddie replied. Sure enough, Norman pulled out the 9-iron and hit it off the tee, just making the fairway. A few moments later he whipped out his driver and nonchalantly knocked his second onto the green. Not only on the green, but twelve feet from the hole. He knocked in the putt.

- Fifty years before Tiger Woods and his Nike commercials,

Moe was bouncing balls off a clubface for fun. He liked to give tournament crowds a laugh by walking along and bouncing at the same time. His record was 194 yards. Once, a spectator bet he couldn't do it 100 times, and was prepared to pay a dollar for every bounce past the ton, if Moe paid a dollar for every bounce short of it. Moe deliberately missed at 184. 'I had to stop because I was holding up the tournament.'

- A few years ago Moe played a round with a reporter at the Royal Oak Golf Club in Florida. He arrived late on the first tee, stuck a ball on a tee, and smashed it away. It shot into the sky but headed straight towards a lake, landing just the other side of a palm tree in front of the water. It looked like it must have found the lake because Moe hit another shot almost immediately. It went over the same spot of the same tree. When he got to his balls they were four feet apart, and six feet from the water. Far from hitting his drives off line, Moe had taken the shortest possible route to the hole and laid up in front of the water in a virtually impossible-to-get-to spot. Having reduced the hole to a drive and a wedge, he knocked the first ball over the lake to six feet from the flag, and the other ball to four feet. The records don't show whether he holed the putts. Like Moe, they probably figured that the interesting bit had already happened.

- Moe's confidence was unswerving. Once, before a round at his home club, Rockway, he was found pulling clubs out of his bag. When asked what he was doing, he replied that because the wind was up that day he knew that he wouldn't need his 5-iron on 6, nor his 4-iron on 10. Basically, he knew every shot he was going to hit that day before the round had started, so why weigh the bag down with clubs he wouldn't need?

- Up until he was twenty-eight Moe was an amateur. When an amateur wins he doesn't get given a six-foot long cardboard cheque, he gets a TV, or a luggage set, or a wristwatch. Or he did in Moe's day. Thing is, how many watches does one wrist need? While they weren't supposed to, most amateurs would sell these prizes so they could get to the next tournament. Moe was no different. Except in one way. Moe used to sell his prize before the tournament had begun.

- Moe's first tournament as a pro was the Los Angeles Open. In the first round he knocked the ball in a green-side bunker and when he heard the crowd moan, told them not to worry, the shot was so easy he could play it one-handed. One fan took him up on that and bet him $10 he couldn't. Moe marched into the bunker, flopped it out with one hand to two feet, and pocketed the money.

- During a clinic, someone put a ball bag about 100 yards down the range and promised they'd donate $5 to charity every time Moe hit the bag. At $100 won, with the bag having been hit with everything from wedges to drivers, the hapless donor begged Moe to stop.

- Another time, Moe gave a clinic to a bunch of folk more anxious to get to the bar than watch a guy with a funny swing. To get their attention Moe announced that the clinic would now begin. He took aim at the practice green eighty-five yards away and knocked his first shot into the hole on the fly. The clinic lasted an hour and a half.

- Moe hits his driver so pure and clean that he rarely disturbs the tee. At one exhibition he hit 146 drives off the same tee before he had to re-peg it into the ground. The tee he uses today is one that he's had since 1989.

- When the mood takes him, Moe keeps his tee in his pocket and uses something else instead. Sometimes, it's a special eight-inch tee. Sometimes, it's the course's wooden tee-marker. And frequently, it's a Coke bottle. In the old days he would delight spectators by doing the Coke bottle trick in the middle of tournaments. (In his first round as a pro, having been warned that the bottle shot would not be allowed, he used the eight-inch tee instead, as they'd forgotten to mention that.) Every now and then, he'd use nothing at all, just dropping the ball on the grass and smashing away. If he was feeling particularly cheeky, he'd step on it first, pushing it into the ground. Then he'd whip out his driver and blast it down the middle, like always.

- At one exhibition, Moe hit 1540 drives in just under seven hours. They all went longer than 225 yards, and all landed inside a marked thirty-yard-wide landing zone.

The pros know. The pros appreciate Moe Norman for the genius that he is. It's only us Sunday hackers who have our heads in the sand.

Take Ben Crenshaw: 'Remarkable. Remarkable. People who've never seen him wouldn't know from someone's description how good he is. You have to see it to believe it. He's slightly unorthodox, but the only thing you have to see is the ball going to the target, every time, every time.'

Paul Azinger: '(Norman) got out of his car and (coach) John Redman said, "Boys, there's the greatest ball-striker who ever lived right there." I looked over at this guy and went "Yeah, right." It was about 120 degrees and he's wearing a long-sleeve turtleneck. He started ripping these drivers *right off the ground* at the 250-yard marker and he never hit one more than 10 yards to either side of it, and he hit at least 50. It was an incredible sight. When he hit irons, he was calling how many times you'd see it bounce after he hit it – sometimes before he hit it – and he'd do it. It was unbelievable.'

Lee Trevino: 'I remember him standing by the range when I won the Canadian PGA. [I was hitting a 5-iron and] I said, "Hey, Moe, these people want to know how good you can hit it." Well, the first one he put the club behind the ball about six inches and he hit the prettiest little draw out about 170 yards. Then another ball with the same amount of draw maybe a foot away from the first. He hit five golf balls and they were in a five-foot circle. I mean Moe could cover the balls he hit with a blanket. There's no question in my mind that Moe Norman would have made it anywhere. In Europe, in the US and beyond. To me he didn't have a picturesque swing, but he's the best ball striker I ever saw come down the pipe. I haven't seen them all, but I don't know how anyone could have hit the ball better than Moe Norman.'

Ken Venturi *(1964 US Open winner, long-time TV commentator, and the world's foremost expert on Ben Hogan's swing*): 'Is Moe Norman the best ball-striker who ever lived? It would be pretty hard to dispute that. Most players see only one shot in a given situation, but Moe always had multiple choice. He'd see probably three ways to play it. Moe had more varied shots than anyone I'd ever seen. Hogan was a static shotmaker, but I think Moe could do more things. Like hitting a driver out of a divot.'

And, to finish, Moe Norman himself: 'Is that pure? Oh man. Hoo boy. Is that pure? Hoo hoo. Never off plane. Watch again. Even a miss is dead straight. Watch again. Oh, it's so simple. Like falling off a log. Hoo man.'

And again: 'I'm the best striker of a ball the world has known. That's not me saying it. Ask all the pros who's the best. Ben Hogan and I are in a different world, which doesn't exist for anyone else trying to hit it pure – dead straight, every time. I'm still waiting for a tournament at midnight.'

Or, to put it another way, 'I hit it so straight, I'm the only guy who can play golf in the dark.'

It wasn't always like this. People weren't always so positive towards Murray 'Moe' Norman, and despite his incredible ability, his is a story as bitter as it is sweet. Growing up in a working class family in Kitchener, Ontario, red-haired Moe was considered an oddball, a misfit and a freak. A naturally shy and sensitive child, he spoke incredibly fast in a high-pitched, sing-songy voice and had a tendency to repeat phrases, which lingers to this day. 'Moe's a schmo, Moe's a schmo … gotta go, gotta go.' Kids being kids, he was picked on and ridiculed all through his school years, which left him feeling miserable, scared, different and unwanted.

Some people, including his family, feel that a lot of his problems stem from an accident he had when he was five, when he was struck in the face by a car after the toboggan he was on went out of control and ended up in traffic. This left the young Moe with frontal lobe damage which would explain a lot of his behaviour. (Repeating yourself and rapid speaking are common traits of brain injury.) Moe's friends, meanwhile, are convinced that he's a higher functioning autistic, likening him to the character Dustin Hoffman played in *Rain Man*. This rings true, for Moe has an incredible gift for numbers. When he was a kid, and despite being bottom of every other class, he was an absolute whizz in maths, working out complicated problems so fast even the teachers were dazzled. Today, he can take you through rounds he played decades ago and tell you every club he hit on every hole, and how many putts he took on the green. Even more astonishing, he can tell you the par and yardage of every hole of every course he has played. Whenever he plays a hole for the first time, he memorises it, and stores the information for possible use in the future.

Sports were a refuge for the young, beleaguered Moe Norman, for they were the only place he felt on a par with the other kids. He had a great eye for a ball and, coupled with an inexhaustible energy, would throw himself into any physical challenge. In the end, though, it was golf that drew him in. He loved that golf was a solitary game, where you did your own thing, without having to rely on team-mates. Here was something he could be good at, but still stay in his own little world.

The great irony, though, is that Moe was irresistibly

drawn to what must surely be the stuffiest, most traditional, most rule-bound game on earth. Yet here was this super-talented golfer, gate-crashing the country club, who could only live by his own rules, and who would never see the world as committees do. Moe into golf just didn't go, and there's no doubt that the golf establishment itself was as responsible as anyone else for Moe's failure to go on and dominate the professional game.

In the beginning, Moe did what every golf-mad kid did. He caddied. And it wasn't long before he was making waves at the Westmount Golf and Country Club. One day, he got stuck caddying for a notorious millionaire skinflint and when, at the end of the round, he got tossed two quarters – the absolute bare minimum for his services – he tossed them right back at the guy, saying 'You need them more than I do.' He then grabbed the man's clubs and started throwing them up a tree. Three of them stayed up there, and Moe got banned for a month. Most of the members loved him though, because he was the best caddie on the books – fast and knowledgeable and supernaturally good at finding a lost ball. Trouble was, Westmount caddies could only play golf on a Thursday, which was no good to the rap-idly-becoming-obsessed Moe.

Rockway was a public course in Kitchener, and it was here that Moe found his spiritual home. And to judge by the amount of time he spent up there, his actual home as well. When he wasn't caddying, he was on the range, pounding balls, and working on his homemade swing. Golf was now his life and, while still the same shy and withdrawn kid, he wasn't afraid of anything where golf was concerned. Once, he found himself caddying in a tournament for a Canadian amateur called Nick Weslock, reckoned to be one of the best amateurs ever to have played the game. The sixteenth at Rockway is a 145-yard par-three and that day the shot was a little into the wind.

'This is a 7-iron shot,' Weslock said.

'No, it's an 8-iron,' Moe insisted.

'You sure?' asked Weslock.

'You hit the 7-iron and you'll carry your bag from here in.'

Weslock swallowed hard, but did as he was told. After all, the kid hadn't mis-clubbed him once all day. He knocked it three feet from the hole and went on to win.

Everyone thinks Ben Hogan is the king of the practisers, but he's got nothing on Moe Norman. During those early Rockway years, Moe would be out there in blazing temperatures that had everyone else hiding in the clubhouse. Usually, it was only darkness that would stop him. He didn't ever seem to tire, and when his hands began to blister and bleed he'd just wipe them on his pants and carry on. Every day he got a step closer to figuring out his swing, and at the same time, practise was a kind of therapy too. He got to work out his frustrations and lose himself in the simple act of hitting ball, after ball, after ball.

At nineteen he had his basic swing down pat (his magic move, as he called it) and he emerged from his cocoon of practice to enter a few events.

Moe must have made a hell of an impression on the unsuspecting Canadian amateur circuit that year. It wasn't just his swing that was different, it was everything. While other players were well-heeled and dapper, Moe was like a freckle-faced, wild-haired urchin. He had a ragged canvas golf bag that was full of holes and only held together at the bottom by carpet tape. Most caddies wouldn't have been seen dead carrying such a bag, but that was okay, for Moe preferred to carry his own clubs. He nearly always wore long sleeve shirts, or turtle-neck sweaters, regardless of how hot it was, and the clashing colours he sported suggested a man who'd just grabbed whatever came to hand that morning. He didn't own any golf shoes so he wore running shoes instead. (His clubs, however, were top-notch; Bobby Jones irons and woods, thanks to a generous Westmount member.) He would roar round the course at high speed, and often, if the pace of play was too slow for his liking, he would lie down on the fairway in protest and pretend to go to sleep. He never took a practice swing and appeared to pay hardly any attention to each actual shot, walking up to his ball and hitting it, almost without breaking stride. From start to finish, Moe's entire shot routine took three seconds. He was even quicker on the greens. And, of course, if at any point he fancied doing his famous Coke bottle trick, well he'd just go ahead and do it. (Having a bottle to hand wasn't a problem; he drank around a case of Cokes a day.)

(There's no doubt that Moe could have achieved more if he had been a better putter. He hit his full shots quickly because he was supremely confident, but he rushed his putts because he couldn't really see the point of putting. It felt wrong to Moe that a three-foot putt should be as important as the 220-yard 3-wood that had put it there in the first place. It didn't seem to be what golf was about and he never really took it seriously. He'd get bored waiting for others to putt and would often just waft his putter one-handed at short putts, missing dozens down the years. 'Miss'em quick, miss'em quick,' he used to say.)

In 1949, he won his first amateur tournament, setting a pattern in more ways than one. For while Moe loved the game, and loved the idea of winning even more, there was one aspect of playing great golf that scared him down to his boots – making a victory speech afterwards. So while everyone waited for the new champ to step up, receive his prize and say a few words, Moe had already hitched a lift back to Rockway, leaving Nick Weslock to pick up the silver salver for him. A scenario that would repeat itself many times in the next few years. Moe's leaving early was exactly the kind of stunt that so angered the men who ran the game, but to Moe it was a no-brainer. He couldn't think of anything more terrifying than being asked a question in public to which he didn't know the answer. Moe feared that he would panic and make a fool of himself, and surely the sponsors wouldn't want that?

The thing was, people didn't understand Moe. He behaved differently to them, and rather than take the trouble to understand the thinking behind his actions, they were quick to judge him instead. Moe was cripplingly shy so if a stranger spoke to him they were apt to get short shrift in return. If he didn't know you, he was afraid of you, but it didn't come across like that.

Golf has always been too solemn a game – all that 'Quiet Please' and studied concentration and being 'in the zone'. Moe would hare round the course chattering merrily away, smiling to one and all with the same happy demeanour every time, whether he was shooting high or low. Sounds a great approach, doesn't it? Except, of course, people thought he wasn't taking the game seriously enough. Moe felt that it wasn't his fault he made the game look so easy, and people should just accept him for what he was. After all, he was a great crowd-puller and he lit up the game with his skills. What more did they want?

Over the next few seasons, Moe played the kind of golf the world very rarely sees. His reputation grew and grew as he regularly slaughtered top-quality amateur fields, winning two-thirds of the tournaments he entered (in one summer he won a cool sixteen out of nineteen events). With no car (and no clue how to drive, anyway) he would hitchhike to and from every event in a series of smash-and-grab raids all over Canada. This colourful character would arrive in town, amaze everyone with his swing and his golf, and be gone again before you could say 'Silver Salver'.

And then Moe won the big one. The 1955 Canadian Amateur Championship. Not only had he officially proved he was his country's No. 1 player, but as the Canadian Amateur Champion he could expect an important letter to drop on his doormat in a few months time. His invitation to play in The Masters, at Augusta.

Playing at Augusta should have been the moment when the world, getting their first good look at Moe, sat up and marvelled at this exciting and charismatic new talent. (The 1956 Masters was only the second one to be televised.) Sadly, it didn't turn out that way.

Like a little kid he got there a week ahead of time and played forty-five holes every day, thrilled at the thought that he would soon be teeing it up with the Hogans, Sneads and Sarazens of this world. And when the first round arrived he made a typical Moe Norman entrance. He was playing in the group in front of Byron Nelson and Gary Middlecoff, the defending Masters champion, and after his partner had hit, the announcer turned his attention to Moe.

'Please welcome to the tee, from Kitchener, Canada, the 1955 Amateur Champion of Canada' – *thwack!* – 'uh, Murray Norman.' The announcer hadn't even said his name yet, but Moe had hit his drive and charged off after it.

From tee to green Moe was his usual dead-eye self but, a lackadaisical putter at the best of times, Augusta's slick greens did for him. He had six three-putts, but still managed to shoot 75, just three over par; an incredible score in the circumstances. The second round was another horror show on the greens, and he turned in a 78. In those days, there was no cut so Moe did what he always did after a round. He headed for the range.

After a bit, Sam Snead sauntered along and stopped to watch Moe. Maybe he didn't know about Moe's swing; maybe he was just trying to be helpful, but he gave Moe a tip about sweeping your long irons. Rather than politely thanking him, then going right back to the way he has always hit his shots, Moe started working on Snead's suggestion. It was if, for the first time, he'd lost faith in his own style. Or perhaps it was because it was the legendary Sam Snead who'd made the suggestion. Whatever the reason, Moe stayed on that range for another four hours, hitting 800 practice balls. Never had he hit such a large amount of balls in such a short space of time. When dusk fell, and Moe stopped to draw breath, his hands were like hamburgers, all bloodied and shredded. It was yet another totally irrational and inexplicable act from a man who seemingly couldn't help but press the self-destruct button.

Moe knew he'd gone too far. He soaked his hands in hot water, but it was too late, the following day they were blistered and raw, and his left thumb had split open. After nine holes of agony, he walked in, unable to hold the club and cursing himself for having ruined his dream trip to the Masters. The green-blazered Masters officials were not happy either, and Moe slunk away from Augusta with his tail between his legs.

The next year, to prove it was no fluke, Moe won the Canadian Amateur Championship again, playing some breathtaking golf along the way. A matchplay tournament, Moe was 31-under par for the week, and over 64 holes of the final and semi-final he was 22-under, with only one bogey. In the semis over the brutish Edmunston course he shot a 9-under par, course record 64, which stands to this day and, ever the scamp, gave his opponent four putts over five feet during their match..

He also got another invite to the Masters but, once again, couldn't get to grips with the greens and shot 78-74. (1957 being the first year The Masters had a cut.)

Storm clouds were waiting for him at home too. The authorities could no longer turn a blind eye over his flagrant and repeated selling of prizes. Nor his trick-shot exhibitions, and the money that people put into a hat afterwards. Nor could they ignore the rumour that clubs were paying him appearance money to play in their tournament and help with travel expenses. If only he'd been more discreet about his dealings, Moe might have been all right, but it wasn't in him to be subtle and soon he was being singled out for breaking the rules of his amateur status. He wasn't the only one, of course, but he was Moe Norman, scourge of official-dom, ignorer of rules and protocol, driver of balls off Coke bottles – and it was time to pay the piper.

Before an official investigation was called, Moe did the only thing he could. He turned pro.

For many of his supporters this was what he should have done years ago. They couldn't wait for Moe to get out there on the PGA Tour and show the world what a star he was, but for Moe it wasn't that simple. He liked amateur golf. It was where his friends were. It was what he knew. For someone with Moe's insecurities the PGA Tour was a scary, threatening place and he was never at his best under those conditions. But he was cornered. They were about to throw the book at him and there was no escape but to renounce his amateur status before they did it first.

Moe played in ten events on the 1959 Winter Tour, making just $1360 in prize money – $1100 of which came from a single fourth place finish. He played the Winter Tour again in 1960 with similar results. He won $1529 to break even on his expenses.

And that was it. He came home and never played on Tour again.

So what went wrong? How could someone so talented fail to make the grade amongst inferior golfers not fit to tuck his shirt in? Well, as ever, it came down to the way Moe was, and the way other people are. The fans loved him but the players never really took him seriously. They knew he had a good game but one look at his appearance, and how fast he played, and the way he talked, and the odd, stunted swing he had, and the goofy things he did on the course, and his goose was cooked. They just felt he wasn't one of them and while the star players did what they could to make him feel accepted, the journeymen, the ones whose livelihoods he was threatening, made it clear that he didn't fit in.

If Moe had had a thicker skin, it wouldn't have mattered, but he didn't. He had an inferiority complex that was barely skin deep, and being patronised by his peers just brought it all to the surface once more.

In the end, he was never really able to be himself. It wasn't so much the curbing of the Coke bottle trick, and things like that, but the everyday stuff he needed to make him tick.

He got lonely. Most of the PGA pros thought he was a loner anyway, but he wasn't at all. Moe needed people to chatter and laugh with, but all his pals were back home, and making new friends was never his strong suit.

He could only play fast. Moe was used to matchplay where you can motor right along, but PGA events were strokeplay where every bad shot cost you money and it paid to be methodical. Play would slow to a crawl and Moe would get fidgety and lose his focus.

He putted differently. With the pace of play so slow, he took more time over his putting because he thought he ought too. It made him an even worse putter, no longer even having his instinct to rely on.

Ken Venturi had his own theory. He reckoned Moe was too gifted for his own good. 'He'd go off on these tangents. He'd never get where he could get geared in for four hours and grind it out and use his talent. He'd drift in and out. He'd be playing and then he'd have to do something different, saying "I'm going to play these different kinds of shots now." He had so much talent, he got a bit bored unless he was doing something with it.'

And there was one other incident that sealed his fate.

During what became his final tournament, Moe was given a public dressing down by some officials and one of the top pros. It was the usual stuff; dress smarter, take a caddie like the others, use a proper tee, blah, blah, blah. If he'd been anyone else, Moe would have shrugged it off, but he felt he'd been rejected and that he would never be wanted. It hurt, and Moe's tactic to avoid pain was to run away from it. So he just upped and left, his dreams of fame and fortune in tatters.

He was still a pro though, and during the 1960s continued to give lessons and exhibitions. Back where he belonged his game flourished once more and there were still weeks where he wreaked havoc on the Canadian circuit. Nineteen sixty-six in particular was a great year for Moe, winning five times that summer and coming second five more.

As the 1970s dawned, Moe was spending summers in Canada and winters in Florida, and even the Canadian authorities were finally beginning to appreciate what a gem they had in Moe Norman. He was invited onto the national team for the odd match – something they wouldn't have dreamed of doing earlier in his career. It was at these events that Moe would get to see the respect he was still held in by the pros that mattered. One minute he'd be practising (no change there then), the next minute Nicklaus would wander over to watch him hit balls, or Player, or Trevino. It was like the world was only just beginning to cotton on to how unique and special he was.

Eventually, Moe lost his enthusiasm for competitive golf, getting much more excited about some of the youngsters he found himself partnered with, encouraging them on as they played. His only thrill seemed to be in attempting impossible shots to protected pins. And if the shot didn't come off, well, as Moe put it with a shrug, 'It's just a walk in the park.'

When Moe turned fifty he wowed them all over again on the Canadian Senior Tour but, much to the exasperation of his friends who thought he could finally make some big money, steadfastly refused to go over to the States and play on their senior circuit. Once bitten, twice shy perhaps, although Moe claims it's simply because he didn't have a sponsor and couldn't afford it.

By the mid-1990s Moe had pretty much dropped off the radar. His friends were worried about what was he going to do with himself and, in turn, how he would make a living.

And then two wonderful things happened.

Wally Uihlein, the CEO and President of Titleist, announced that, in recognition of his ball-striking skills, the company would pay Moe Norman $5000 a month for the rest of his life. All Moe has to do is be himself.

And a man called Jack Kuykendall hired Moe to spread the word of Natural Golf – a swing virtually identical to Norman's that Kuykendall had devised without any knowledge of Moe and his theories. Kuykendall is committed to getting the golfing world to change their swing habits, and can't think of a finer spokesman than the now grey-haired kid from Kitchener, Ontario.

It is ironic that the seventy-five-year-old Moe Norman now commands more awe and respect than was ever afforded him in his heyday.

But he doesn't mind. After decades of uncertainty, he's finally being allowed to spend all day doing what he loves most.

Hitting balls.

And drinking Cokes. (These days, caffeine-free.)

CHAPTER EIGHTEEN: THE SECRET OF GOLF

Ah, the secret of golf.

What better way to finish than to reveal The Big One.

Now, over the years some serious golfing luminaries have chucked their own personal theories into the ring, and I could give you a very long list right here, comprising the valuable thoughts of those who should surely know best.

I am not going to. For the simple reason that every single one of their theories is different, sometimes startlingly so, and you come away thinking that, actually, nobody really knows anything. Which rather defeats the object and, in turn, will make you doubt what I have to say, and we can't have that.

The other thing is, I'm not sure these people really do know best. They're wonderful golfers, for sure, but that's just the problem. When they say they've got the secret of golf, what they really mean is, when your swing, stance and grip are correct, and you already play golf to a terrific standard, then this is what you should do to give yourself the best chance of scoring to your sub-par potential.

Well, I'm sorry, but professionals are very different creatures to the rest of us. (Backspin, anyone? Taking off your glove to putt? Insisting that the bunker shot is the easiest shot in golf?) And multiple major-winners are yet more different still. I have next to nothing in common with these people – I don't even wear a visor – and, as harsh as it sounds, I cannot trust them to know what's best for me and my game. And you shouldn't either.

In order to hit a good golf shot you have to do dozens of different things correctly. You know the drill: grip; stance; address; posture; ball placement; grip pressure; waggle; visualisation of the shot; golf ball made from the latest gravity-defying chemical compound – and we haven't even started the backswing yet. If I were you – and I am – what I'd want to know is, all things being equal, what's the really, really, *really* important one? Or ones, even. The top tip that can best help the average golfer.

We've all seen Jim Furyk play, so you don't have to be Leadbetter, or even Bergerac, to work out that swing plane is probably not the be all and end all for an effective golf swing.

So what is?

Well, before we get down to the nitty-gritty, and in the interests of a fair and balanced perspective, there is one other point to make. A few years back a Sunningdale member called Tony Howard achieved a quantum leap in his game and, for two or three years, became pretty much the best player in the club, winning a number of its most prestigious scratch competitions and posting some glorious sub-70 scores into the bargain. This was lovely to see. Partly because he is one of the nicest guys in the whole club, but also because his handicap, before it dropped like a stone and he began winning anything he cared to enter, was the same as mine is now (6) and I couldn't help but think that if he could do it, so could I.

I was chatting with him in the bar one day and, somewhat brazenly, came right out and asked him how it was that he could go from being a decent 6-handicapper to a consistent par-frightener, in what seemed like the blink of an eye, In short, what was the secret of his success?

(When I was a bit younger I used to do a bit of acting. I hope to God that when I heard his answer that day I was able to disguise my disappointment.)

'Practice', he said, matter-of-factly.

Bugger.

No magic moves; no mental tricks; no extra Shredded Wheat. Just practice – the one aspect of the game that is beyond me.

So then, in much the same way that an advertisement for an investment trust has to tell you that the value of shares may go down as well as up, I must advise you that any secret of golf you may discover in the following pages will only be fully effective if your muscles are taught the aforementioned secret through the tedious and repetitive act of practice. It's a bitch, but there you are.

Right, the secret of golf, then.

Well, first things first – there's two secrets, not one. And the reason there are two secrets is obvious. Good golf comes in two guises, neither of which can be ignored.

Hitting it well.

And hitting it straight.

Let's take the less sexy one first.

Hitting it Straight

I have always been a wild hitter, right from the word go. This came hand in hand with trying to smash hell out of the ball. In fact, I was so in love with hitting the ball hard that for many years I figured that not knowing where it was going was actually, all things considered, a pretty reasonable price to pay for the occasional, eye-popping, gasp-inducing long-range missile. Me and Mark T actually had a catchphrase, coined as a result of our uncanny knack of hitting the thing anywhere and everywhere.

It would have been great
if it had been straight.

(Beat that, Brucie. It even rhymed – what more do you want from a catchphrase?)

I can't tell you how many times we looked at each other and said those words, as wood after wood, and iron after iron, was despatched miles wide of its intended target. And we weren't even joking; we really did think that we were being hard done by; that the hard bit was hitting it well, and that it was somehow unfair that we couldn't hit it straight, and not really our fault at all.

And then a few things all seemed to happen at once. I reached my thirties; I got married; I had kids, I forsook heavy metal, I started playing golf a lot less so each game became more precious; I grew up a bit; I decided it was a bit silly to keep trying to hit the ball so damn hard, and then – I think it was a Tuesday – I was hit by a sudden, blinding realisation. The sort that makes you slap your forehead with the palm of your hand.

It even came to me in italics:

There is a reason why the golf pros on TV swing like they do, and that's because it's the correct way to play golf.

And sure enough, there was one thing that the pros did – every single last one of them – that I had never, ever done, not even once. (Ooh, is it me, or is it getting quite exciting now?)

Here it is, then, without further faffing around – The Secret of Hitting a Golf Ball Straight

– Turn your hips on the downswing, so that your belt buckle is facing the hole as you hold your finish –

Trust me.

Turn your hips on the downswing, so that your belt buckle is facing the hole as you hold your finish.

And why is this such a magic move? Because it means you cannot 'steer' or 'force' your shot. Turning your hips (think of it as clearing your hips out the way) ensures that the club stays on the straightest line through the ball, and that the ball then simply 'gets in the way' of the middle of your swing and the straightness of the shot just takes care of itself.

It takes a bit of getting your head around – surely you should try and hit every shot in the direction you want it to go – but that's exactly the point. Golf is a game of opposites. If you want a pitch shot to rise up sharply, you hit down on it: if you want the ball to move to the right, you cut across it to the left; and if you want the ball to go where you want it, the last thing you do is try and steer it in that direction.

All I know is that this little move has totally transformed my game, and I'm sure it can do something for you. Remember that scuff-smother-squirter I told you about? The one that went forty-five degrees left? Haven't seen it round these parts for years now. But the really joyous bit; the time when this move comes into its own, is on the first tee. These days I can go a long time between games; frequently weeks, occasionally months. It doesn't matter. I stand on that first tee – the golfer's equivalent of a precipice's edge – and my sweet, gorgeous hip-turn just does its thang.

Imagine for a moment how that feels. You get to the golf club late; you wolf down a somewhat stewed coffee from the pot at the bar; you put on your golf shoes – still a bit muddy from last time – you stroke a few practice putts and then you stand next to the first tee, waiting your four-ball's turn to go off. You take a few practice swings, which feel pretty damn creaky, but you do at least remember to do that hip turn thing, and suddenly you notice that the club's high-rollers are on the tee after you and this isn't good 'cos they're all off a category one handicap and hate being held up, and next thing you know you're putting your tee in the ground and it's your turn and there's a dozen pairs of eyes looking at you and the final practice swing you take is way too hurried and you know it is and as you look down the hole the fairway seems as thin as a ruler whereas the rough looks the size of Rodney Marsh … sorry, Romney Marsh, and it always takes ages to find anything hit in there but then you think no, come on, just trust the hip turn, just clear those bloody hips, and you do, you commit to it, you make it happen and stone me if the ball doesn't go almost dead straight and you've got such a lovely finish to your swing that you showboat a little and hold the position a couple of seconds longer than you should.

You then do what is officially known as the coolest thing in golf; the thing that the pros do when they've hit a good shot; the thing that makes you hate them and love them all at the same time.

You don't bother looking at the ball while it's in the air.

Hell, why would you? It's gone pretty much straight down the middle, it can take care of itself and you've got the rest of your life to be getting on with. While the ball is barely halfway through its flight you're already picking up the tee and walking towards your discarded headcover. Meanwhile, everyone else is thinking that you have the casual, uninterested look of a man who knew he was going to do that all along.

And all because of a little hip-turn.

The first tee at Rye is the acid test for any swing theory. There are rolling mounds in front of you that effectively obscure most of the hole and, because it's a links course, there are no trees in the distance to act as sighters. All you can see of the hole is the left hand edge of it, and while this is helpful, just a few yards to the left of that is a main road that stretches the length of the hole and scares the shit right out of you. Basically, you have to aim to the right of that left edge, ignore the road, and commit to the shot. Yeah, right.

I've been a member at Rye for about five years now (having moved down to that part of the country a decade ago) which means that every time I've hit that tee shot I've employed the hip-turn theory. Other than trying not to swing too hard it's the only swing thought I give myself on the first tee. I haven't once hit the ball on to the road, nor have I even come close. In five years. And this from a man who was plagued by a hook for twenty years. Sure, sometimes I get a bit too defensive and push it right a bit, but that's about as bad as it gets. Standing on that tee is like going to church and having your faith reaffirmed. Every time I think the same thoughts. *'It's my first shot of the day, I haven't practised, I didn't eat my greens as a child, surely the old hip-turn isn't going to work again. (THWACK!) Well, blow me down, would you look at that?'*

Occasionally, I play courses that I played a lot in my teens and twenties and, as I stand on some of the tees, the ones where there's trouble left and right, I get a kind of flashback and I can remember what I felt all those years ago.

Fear.

The fear and anxiety that comes with not knowing where the hell you're going to hit the ball, or how on God's earth you're going to find the fairway.

Final piece of evidence: a couple of months after I'd joined the Church of The Holy Hip-Turn I played a round with one of the assistant pros at Sunningdale. If memory serves we played for something small, but not insignificant, like twenty quid. (I used to find it a good idea to play one of the assistants every now and then. It's always good to play with good golfers, and I thought that if we played for a little bit of money it might toughen up my matchplay.) I concentrated hard and made sure I executed my new and exciting hip move on every shot. After all, you don't want to play a stinker in front of a pro.

I played the first nine in 33 shots – the only time I've ever scored that low. I then parred the tenth hole and found myself 6-up at the halfway hut against a professional golfer; and 2 under par to boot. Sadly, as the very real possibility of a first ever 60-something around Sunningdale dawned on me, I got a bit scared and my game went as wobbly as a jelly, moulded in the shape of my tummy. But I still comfortably won the match, and I owe it all to you-know-what.

Watch golf. Watch the pros. Get Sky, and pay close attention as those hips rotate and groin after groin gets proudly thrust forward. Then turn over from the Men and Motors channel, and find Sky Sports instead. C'mon, this is serious.

Anyway, there it is. The secret to hitting the ball straight, according to a chubby, middle-aged, under-achieving, six-handicapper.

What have you got to lose?

Other than a brand new Srixon surlyn.

Hitting it Well

I have a theory as to why golf is such an addiction to so many people. It's only a hunch, but it's mine, and I like it.

Essentially, golf is the furthest Man can propel an object using his own energy and strength. It used to be the arm-throw that sent a ball the furthest, but then along came golf and with only the aid of a bent stick, all of a sudden Man could send that sucker way out there. (Catapults don't count, by the way – the energy coming from the stretched rubber, as opposed to the human body.) As I'm sure you know, there is something intensely pleasing, in a primal sort of way, for your body to send a golf ball soaring off into the far distance, and on the rare occasions it also goes in the same direction you intended, you cannot help but feel powerful and magical. To hit a little white ball with a fairway 3-wood, and land it on a small green 250 yards from where you are, is to experience one of life's giddier moments. And it probably means you'll win the hole as well.

In other words, Man has a basic need – a primal urge – to propel an object away from him as far as it can go. It's no different to his need to procreate. And it's why we cannot be blamed for our obsessive quest to hit a golf ball further and further. We have no choice; we are merely prisoners of our own make-up.

Which brings us – much earlier than anyone could possibly have dared hope for – to The Secret of Hitting It Well. All I would say, by way of an introduction, is this: isn't it interesting how sometimes the really important things we should know are also the most boring?

The Secret of Hitting a Golf Ball Well

– Keep your hands nice and firm at the top of your backswing –

I'll repeat that.

Keep your hands nice and firm at the top of your backswing.

If you think about it, it makes a lot of sense. As we stand at address we only actually have one objective: to take the club away from the ball, swing it all around our body, and return it to the ball exactly the same way it was when it started. If you collapse your hands at the top, even a little bit, you are now going to have to try and 'find' the ball when you arrive back down. You are trusting to luck and the good nature of The God of Golf (and we all know what a sadistic swine he is).

Whereas, if your arms are fully extended when you start your downswing – like they were when you took them away in the first place – the club has no option but to greet the ball at the same place it left it.

Think of the straight, unbending, uncollapsing hand of a clock, first pointing down at 6, then swinging round past 12 and stopping at 3, then coming all the way back again to give 6 a fearful whack. Then, when that doesn't help, just think 'high' hands. If your hands are high at the top of your backswing then, ipso facto, it's impossible for them to also be floppy. (A little while back, Davis Love III was reckoned to be the longest hitter around. He was also the man with the 'highest' hands in golf: I've seen a photo of him in this position and it is almost freakish how high they are. The only downside? He's always being asked to get jars down from shelves.)

As ever, I can only tell you about the things that make my game tick and then ask you to have faith that our games are, actually, not too dissimilar. And all I know is, whenever I'm hitting it a bit dodgy I just concentrate on getting those hands nice and firm at the top and, as if by magic, I *immediately* start hitting them sweet and crisp.

And that's it: The Secret of Hitting It Well.

Only … not quite.

The truth is that not only does The Secret of Golf come in two parts, but so does The Secret of Hitting It Well. I'm sorry, I tried to leave this second bit out but I just couldn't; sometimes the golf swing's like that. If it helps, I promise we won't spend too long on it. Look at it this way: if you were planning to try out The Secret of Hitting It Well, it will work even better if you add the following advice to the mix. It's like putting nutmeg on top of an egg custard – you don't have to but you'd be daft not to.

The good news is that The Secret of Hitting It Well (Part Two) is not so much something you should do, as something you shouldn't.

The Secret of Hitting it Well (Part Two)

Don't try and hit the ball too hard.

You guessed it.

Don't try and hit the ball too hard.

A true story: Sam Snead, the legendary American golfer of the 1950s and 1960s, had been kitted out with a new driver by his club manufacturer and, as part of his promotional duties, was obliged to give the odd exhibition after a tournament was over. The crowds would gather and Sam would delight them with a blinding display of his shot-making skills, which at some point or other would include a few shots with his brand-new driver. He'd be sure to mention the clever people who'd made it and he'd go on to show his audience just how far he could hit it with his new beast.

One day, he decided to do a comparison. He pulled out his old driver so he could show everyone how far it was out-driven by his new club. He teed it up and, to help prove the point, gave it an especially easy swing, which, since Snead is universally regarded as having the laziest, easiest swing ever granted to a golfer, must have been barely more than a pat on the ball's behind.

The ball flew off the clubface and went for miles and miles, eventually landing way past his normal driving distance. Try as he might, his brand new, super-duper, big-boy driver couldn't get anywhere near the little poke with his old one.

His club sponsors were not amused.

Now, if even Sam Snead can make the mistake of equating distance and quality of strike with power and effort expended, it's hardly surprising that the rest of us do too.

Do you ever have those days where you can't seem to get the ball going? You feel like you're swinging okay, but the ball just doesn't stay in the air the way it should. What do you do? If you're anything like me, you try and hit it harder, in order to hit it better. Does it help? Does it, my fanny.

The trouble with being told not to try and hit the ball too hard is that it feels like someone's trying to take the fun out of the game. It's like teacher telling you not to run in the corridor. But the reality is that swinging well within yourself gives the 2736 working parts of your swing the best possible chance of all coming together correctly 'at the point of impact' (as they say on the instruction videos). We don't need to hit the ball hard, we just need to hit it sweetly. The irony being that we have never had clubs at our disposal more suited to doing exactly that, than we do at the minute. Thanks to the staggering leaps in golf club technology of late, never have our bent sticks been more capable of propelling a golf ball. So why do we still feel the need to get our lunging bodies in on the act as well?

A few years back I conducted a golfing experiment. Standing on the first tee of the New Course at Sunningdale I made a promise to myself. This would be a round where I would hit every single shot *gently*. I wouldn't just swing within myself, I would slow my swing down to the point where it was like I was only trying to hit the ball halfway. And when I said every shot, I meant every shot: chips, drives, pitches, bunker shots, putts, fairway 1-irons – the lot. And, most importantly of all, it didn't matter how I played. However I hit it, no matter how it came off the clubface, I was to hit the next shot just as easy. Even if I hadn't struck one decent shot in the whole of the first nine holes, I was to smile the smile of the righteous and keep right on doing what I was doing. Even if I came to the last desperately needing a par-four to break a hundred and avoid humiliation, I was to stick to my guns, and my plan, come what may.

I had a 73. Gross.

Round the New, considerably the longer of the two courses.

Ridiculously … stupidly … inexplicably … I have never repeated the exercise. Perhaps, deep down, I don't want to be a good golfer. Who knows why we do the things we do?

So please, take the word of a golfing nobody. If you want to hit it well, don't hit it hard.

(Did I mention that golf is a game of opposites?)

Hang On, What's This?

I said a few pages back that the secret of golf was actually two secrets – The Secret of Hitting It Straight, and The Secret of Hitting It Well. Well, if I'm honest, there is one more secret – The Mother and Father of All Secrets – and if anything could lay claim to the title of The Secret of Golf, it's this one.

Yes, I know, I'm pushing my luck now, and I do feel bad about not mentioning this sooner, but I was worried it might make for a rather confusing and off-putting beginning of a chapter.

Hello and welcome to The Secret of Golf. Please be advised that The Secret of Golf is actually three different secrets, the first two dealing with a) Straightness of Direction, and b) Crispness of Strike – secret b) also boasting a sub-secret b)2 regarding Speed of Swing, without which the application of secret b) cannot be successfully implemented – and the third secret being the secret by which every aspect of a successful golf swing shall rest, including secrets a) and b).

Now you're here however, I'm rather hoping that you'll have a kind of 'I've come this far, I might as well plough on' mindset. So, just in case I've still got you, I'll plough on too.

Golf is a difficult game; that much we know. How difficult? Let's seek refuge in statistics.

Only 22% of golfers regularly score better than 90.

Only 6% of men regularly break 80.

Only 1% of golfers shoot par or better.

The average score among all men and women is 100.

Which is all very well, but why is it so? Why is golf so

difficult? What is it about the game that makes it so hard to be anything other than not very good? It's not like golfers don't know *how* to play; all the information and guidance is available everywhere they look. (It's one of the reasons I stopped buying golf magazines. It suddenly dawned on me that I was buying the same read again, and again, and again. How to split those fairways; how to cure that slice/hook/shank/top/dunch; how to beat those first tee nerves; how to putt like the pros; how to chip like Mickelson; how to swing like Ernie; how to win at matchplay; how to make your mind the fifteenth club in your bag; how to hit the recovery shots that you face all the time because you keep hitting it into trouble, even though this can't help but suggest that you're probably not good enough actually to hit the recovery shots we're about to show you; etc., etc. True, I could just read the articles, but how interesting is an interview with Retief Goosen really going to be?)

Maybe it's because golf is one of the few ball games whose ball doesn't move. As mentioned earlier, all other sports – I can only think of snooker that bucks the trend – are reactive. The ball comes to you and you have to react to it; sometimes in a split-second, sometimes longer. Your skills become instinctive. The golfer, on the other hand, has all the time in the world to play his shot, and even longer to think about it beforehand, as he has to walk up to hundreds of yards between each one.

And when he arrives, the ball just sits there; an accusing eyeball, taunting, goading and waiting. It's not going anywhere until you hit it, but now, in one of two ways, your head just isn't right for the job. It's either too empty, or too full.

Too empty and you don't concentrate properly on the next shot. You've had too much time on your hands; you've been chatting; you've been thinking about that report; you've been trying to find that course planner, which should be somewhere in your bag from the last time you played here. Small wonder you can't pull your brain together to hit a good shot.

Too full and your mind gets cluttered with stuff; how this is a shot that you never hit well; how you can't afford to drop another stroke on the way out; how you must remember all those things you've been practising. Hardly surprising you hit a shot as fat as your head.

No. The fact that the ball doesn't move probably doesn't help, but it's not the reason why the game is so hard. Golf is a ferociously difficult game because there's something we don't do when we play it. Something that the pros have forced themselves to do, which is why they don't find the game too hard, but that the rest of us just find too unnatural to execute repeatedly.

You won't like it.

The Ultimate Secret of Golf: No, Really.

– We have to force ourselves not to immediately look up after we've hit the ball –

Or, to put it another way …

Keep your head down.

No, please, surely not. Not the ol' 'keep your head down' cliché. Surely The Secret Of Golf is more mysterious and Zen Buddhist than that. Surely it's something that's so wise we can't even understand it. Ben Hogan … he had it right

... he knew. Something about having to supinate your left kidney on the backswing, and pronate your right kidney on the follow-through. That's more like it. Complete gobbledygook. A secret that only a genius could discover.

Anyway, who are you, Russell? What do you know? How many tournaments have you won? Or even entered? Just because you're called R. Russell doesn't make you Raymond Russell, the PGA professional – an expert in his field with a well-earned right to give advice, as opposed to a non-achieving, self-deluding (rank) amateur with a pocketful of three-quarter-baked theories.

Have you finished? Are you done? Can we continue now?

Just answer me one question: do *you* keep your head down? By which, I don't mean do you tuck your head down into your neck, or do you keep your head still? I mean do you keep looking down at the ball after you've hit it; when it's no longer there; when the shot is on its merry way and your hands and arms have long since swept through the ball?

In short, do you commit yourself to the shot without peeking too early for where the ball has gone?

There is every chance you don't, I'm afraid. This doesn't make you a bad person, just someone whose body doesn't automatically do something that is unnatural in the first place. For this is the big thing problem: the most important bit of the golf swing is also the hardest to consistently execute.

Be honest, you like lifting your head; you want to lift your head; you do lift your head. And why wouldn't you?

It's the most natural thing in the world. Everything else is coming up – your club; your hands; your arms – it's hardly surprising your head wants to join in the fun. And anyway, there's a ball to watch out for. Quite rightly, you want to know where it's going and whether your hopes for the shot have been dashed or rewarded. Who wouldn't sneak a peek?

So yes, no jury would convict you for allowing your head to lift. But you can bet your sweet bippy they would shake their heads and tut a bit.

As unnatural as it is, this head down thing *is* the golf swing. It's what allows the 'hitting it straight' and the 'hitting it well' to happen. It's a letting go of the shot; it's a letting it happen; it's a trusting it. In his excellent little book, *On Golf* Timothy O'Grady refers to how his father described this facet of the game. It has never been summed up better.

All golfers should hit the ball with 'controlled abandon'.

Controlled abandon. Isn't that great?

Technically speaking, I must confess that I don't really know why this non-move, this 'controlled abandon' is so vital. I'll leave that to the swing doctors. I just know when something feels exquisitely right. I just know what the truth is, when I'm lucky enough to stumble across it.

To be fair, I should make mention of what some of you are already thinking. There are, actually, two pros who always lift their head as they hit the ball. Annika Sorenstam and David Duval: one, an Open champion; the other, the best woman golfer in the modern game. The explanation for this anomaly? Well, there is no explanation for Annika Sorenstam, but then there wouldn't be, even if she didn't look up early. What's the explana-

tion for Jack Nicklaus being so much better than everyone else? Or Tiger Woods possibly being even better than that? With some people the normal rules just don't apply.

And as for David Duval, well, he is currently in a slump of heartbreaking proportions from which he may never return as a true force again, and I suspect it may be because of this flaw in his swing. After a slow start to his career, it seems he has been grant- ed only a tantalisingly short burst of other-worldly brilliance, but he leaves us with the memories of a five-year stretch where he won trophies with ease and, on one sun-kissed day in 1999, at the Bob Hope Chrysler Classic, played a round of tournament golf in 59 shots (a feat achieved by only three other people; one of whom being ... you've guessed it ... Annika Sorenstam). I have yet to hear a finer and more gracious speech than the one Duval gave after winning our Open and I pray that he comes back with all guns blazing and shows me up for the blundering old fool that I am.

Anyway, there you have it, 'The Ultimate Secret Of Golf: No, Really', and a few other delicious serving sugges- tions to help you enjoy golf at its tastiest. On the one hand I remind you that they are just the homespun hunches of a serial underachiever, but at the same time I beg you to give them a bash.

Who knows, if I started practising, maybe I'd do them more often, too?

THANKS AND ACKNOWLEDGEMENTS

Thanks to:

Half Man Half Biscuit. Stars in my eyes.

Geoff Davis at Probe Plus for being all give.

Graham Coster for advice, support and going with my idea for the cover.

Bill McCreadie for being, quite by chance, a golfer.

Ayşe Altinok for her brilliant illustrations

Acknowledgements must go to:

Tim O'Connor's terrific book *The Feeling of Greatness. The Moe Norman Story* (Master Press)

Rick Reilly's insightful article on Ian Baker-Finch's fall from grace.

Jock Howard's brilliant piece on Seve Ballesteros's epic Ryder Cup match.

These fine golf writers and their accounts of these amazing stories should be read by as many people as possible.

I can strongly recommend Tim O'Connor's book to anyone whose interest in Moe Norman has been sparked. The account I have written barely scratches the surface and the book really should be read for the full, fascinating story. (My advice is to buy it online as it's not the kind of book you can pluck off the shelves at W. H. Smith – more's the pity.)